Virtual Gods

Tal Brooke
GENERAL EDITOR

HARVEST HOUSE PUBLISHERS
Eugene, Oregon 97402

Cover by Terry Dugan Design, Minneapolis, Minnesota
Cover illustration by Frank Ordaz

VIRTUAL GODS

Copyright © 1997 by Tal Brooke
Published by Harvest House Publishers
Eugene, Oregon 97402

Library of Congress Cataloging-in-Publication Data

Brooke, Tal—
    Virtual gods / Tal Brooke, general editor.
       p.   cm.
    Includes bibliographical references and index.
    ISBN 1-56507-620-6
    1. Computers—Religious aspects—Christianity.   I. Brooke, Tal.
  BR115.C65V57 1997   96–45435
  239'.9—dc21   CIP

Printed in the United States of America.

97   98   99   00   01   02   03   / BF /   10   9   8   7   6   5   4   3   2   1

Contents

92607

Introduction
Tal Brooke

More than once, a giant man-made beast has stood in the town square of history with the claim that it could change the world. In its bargain, it offered people something unique that they considered invaluable while firing their imaginations with the wonders it could perform. If it succeeded, the people would be compelled to magnify it to greatness while giving it the world to change in return. Such a beast entered history early in the last century. If we can understand it, we can also understand the beast that now inhabits the town square of history.

If you asked people in the early 1800s what machine had recently appeared that was changing their world, they would tell you it was the giant steam locomotive. In its heyday, nothing else captured the public imagination quite like the train. It became almost a national obsession with its power to travel great distances and move cargo across the land. Part of the train's allure, on the human end, was the thrill and mystique of the great railway journey so often described by the great writers and poets over the past century—from Mark Twain, Carl Sandburg, John Steinbeck, right up to Paul Theroux (author of *The Great Railway Bazaar*).

Consider the timeless image of the grand nineteenth-century freight trains thundering through small-town rural America with awed onlookers wishing they could climb aboard, on the wave of an impulse, and ride across America's vast expanse. The giant hissing locomotive was something that could take them to exciting places beyond the colorful descriptions handed down by travelers. It could take them through real country—into the wide-open prairies of Montana and Nebraska, the high mountain passes of Colorado, past the huge riverboats rolling down the Mississippi, through the country of Louisiana, and finally on to such great cities as San Francisco, New York, and Boston. During the train journey, the texture of life would unfold outside the car window as scenery, dialects, fashion, and weather changed constantly to form a rich narrative of life.

The romantic mystique of the locomotive journey viewed the traveler as expanding with each journey. Railway travel created rich perspective by quickly telescoping many of life's points of reference. The journey itself became a kind of exotic and liberating rite of passage. If urbane and sophisticated people became that way by having far more points of reference than ordinary folk—much of it gained through travel—*so could others.* And the same idea of inward expansion through travel remains to this day. At its heyday, the train was the beast in the center of the town square.

The train continues to be exciting—the point of Paul Theroux's best-selling narratives. But other mechanical beasts have filled the town square of history since the era of the railroad. Some have been smaller, such as the television and the automobile. Others have been far larger, such as the space shuttle and the Atlas rocket (seen through the eye of the television by most of today's onlookers).

Today, however, a new mechanical giant looms imposingly in the town square. It has entered our world with as much fanfare as the locomotive of the last century, dazzling the imaginations of those standing at the end of the twentieth century.

This new mechanical giant is called cyberspace. The inhabitants of today's global village are looking upon this new leviathan with growing amazement and expectation. Truly, it is the beast at the end of the twentieth century.

If we recall, one of the "miracles" of the train was that it carved up the world, for the first time connecting villages, towns, cities, and even nations. Now cyberspace is connecting the world in a wholly new way. Its omnipresent hardware already covers the earth like a vast neural network. The electronic components of cyberspace literally crisscross and mesh around the surface of the planet, creating an immense human-computer interface. The Internet is only a part of it—a starting point.

Many believe that the present beast will take the human race on a journey through far more exotic terrain than its counterpart of the last century. Many—the youth above all—look at cyberspace in wonder. The fascination of our youth with cyberspace was the inspiration for William Gibson's novel, *Neuromancer*. Gibson passed a digital arcade and saw the new generation reflecting the electronic digital world of computers as colored light and patterns rippled across their faces while they went on imaginary journeys in the arcade. This represented the crudest beginnings of virtual reality. And, indeed, this vision had the future written all over it.

Cyberspace, however, deals not only with travel, but with knowledge and information as well. Beyond the elements it has in common with the railway, cyberspace has even greater affinities with one of the greatest beasts ever to enter history—the printing press. The press inaugurated the original information explosion. It also occupied the town square for hundreds of years.

The printing press was a thing of wonder. The Gutenberg press stormed the world in the early fifteenth century and opened an unprecedented information gateway into the heart of the medieval world, thrusting history into the next age, the Renaissance. For centuries the vast cross-section of people had lived in the darkness of the Middle Ages. Serfs and artisans who were illiterate and ignorant suddenly had access to knowledge and information that was never before available. This single invention changed the social order forever, intersecting human need and human vulnerability while firing the imaginations of people with the wonders it could perform.

Now, on the eve of the next millennium, cyberspace is bringing change in the wind—global thinking and global technology—with amazing synchronicity. Asked at the start of 1997 what big news loomed ahead for the coming year and beyond, the editor of *Time* magazine stated that without a doubt cyberspace and the digital revolution would set the course of the world into the future (*Larry King Show*, CNN, January 3, 1997). This is not just the "smoke and mirrors" of media hype or a new fad, as some claim, but something that has left a tangible footprint across the earth.

Why this immense effort to wire the earth? Is it blind curiosity, or the endless hunger for knowledge? Is something eating away at the soul of man that cannot stop until some hunger is satisfied—maybe a hunger that started in Eden? And where will this quest take us—this limitless hunger for knowledge and experience? Are there other reference points in history that might give us a handle on today's quest?

As in the days of Babel, when men built the great tower with a view to storming heaven, we are today storming heaven once again. Beyond the ceramic, metal, and silicon building blocks of the present undertaking is the ageless desire to push the human race toward new realms of consciousness and human potential. Like the ancient Tower of Babel, the present undertaking is a quest for global unity—even a return to one language, as once existed on the ancient plains of Shinar.

Cyberspace is a beast with unique promises. It portends to be an instrument that can amuse, educate, and expand the boundaries of knowledge and experience. Yet, the very instrument that can invade the mind enough to bring a cornucopia of sensate delights could also enter the hidden recesses of the mind and its most private thoughts. As well, it could have the power to corrupt, deceive, control, police, and perhaps even enslave someday. It is not an instrument to be taken lightly.

When the door into digital history is fully opened it will be a one-way affair. We can never retreat back to the moment before the door opened. That is the nature of such historical doors, as John Milton illustrated in *Paradise Lost*—the first door being in Eden, causing history to cascade.

As we behold cyberspace, we do not want to enter the next age blindly, being carried into some technological future—a kind of Babylon of wires and electrodes—having been told we were destined for some utopian promised land. If the emerging digital frontier promises to bring heaven on earth, as some futurists boast, we must look at other challenges that lie ahead. We must see what lessons history has shown us in the past so we might resist the terrible dictate of George Santayana who repeatedly warned that "those who cannot remember the past are condemned to repeat it."[1]

We must therefore peer across this vast new electronic horizon with the help of a source older than time itself.

— Tal Brooke
Berkeley, California

PART ONE

Cyberspace—
The New Frontier

1

CYBERSPACE: STORMING DIGITAL HEAVEN

Tal Brooke

OVERVIEW

This chapter provides a panoramic view of cyberspace—what it is and how it "feels." It portrays what it is like to experience the various elements of cyberspace: from the Internet with its World Wide Web to virtual reality. It also unveils the engines that power this technology. It shows how cyberspace has grown from its earliest beginnings to the present—and where it is headed. Only then can we appreciate the need to plumb the depths of this electronic ocean—going through the inviting and dazzling outward ripples to those deeper regions that will mold the future.

A vast formless, machine is quickly wrapping itself around the earth like a "virtual glove." It is being built from an endless array of electronic components whose power, range, and size is far greater than the sum of its parts, which weave across the planet like a neural network. This titanic but largely hidden structure is the nervous system of "cyberspace." Like the human nervous system, much of it lies underground, hidden in the flesh of the earth.

For the first time, this maze of electronic hardware extends the human nervous system across the globe. Its potential for altering the course of human history could echo that of the Gutenberg printing press which, for the first time in history, provided books to the masses. Until then, only royalty, the church, the aristocracy, and the academy had books—unique, rare, and penned by human hands. With the press, literacy expanded geometrically through this public conduit of information and ideas. Medievalism and feudalism were replaced by the Renaissance as the social order of the West changed. Today, computers, cyberspace, and the information superhighway (the Internet) could again change the social order, catapulting present-day society fully into globalism as spatial distances collapse between previously divided groups.

The more rudimentary ancestor of cyberspace began in the last century with the telegraph machine laboriously sending out pulses of Morse code along analog wires at so many words per minute. Later came the analog telephone system for voice transmission, allowing significantly more words per minute with the added quality of mood and personality infused into the transmission. The telephone started the great task of wiring the globe. Then microwave towers, satellites, and grand trunk cable emerged on the scene to make possible the transmission of vast amounts of information across continental divides. Computer data entered this bit-stream. More recently fiber-optic cable has come on the scene to replace copper wire. This amounted to replacing a digital capillary tube (the copper wire) with an oil pipeline (fiber optic), upping the transfer rate, by analogy, from thumbnail amounts to millions of gallons per minute.

The powerful hardware that awakens the mechanical nervous system of cyberspace is the computer, the final interface with the human nervous system through eyes, ears, hands, and brains. Yet the hardware is lifeless without the human interface. Consciousness is the key.

In the words of *Time* special editor Philip Elmer-Dewitt, wires and cables and microwaves are not really cyberspace. They are the means of conveyance, not the destination; they are the information superhighway, not the bright city lights at the end of the road. "Cyberspace, in the sense of being 'in the same room,' is an experience, not a wiring system. It is, like Plato's plane of ideal forms, a metaphorical space, a virtual reality."[1] Yet this new technology is only in its early hours of infancy on the earth.

The term "cyberspace" was coined by William Gibson, a 44-year-old American science fiction writer living in Vancouver. Wandering past the video arcades around Vancouver's Granville Street in the early 1980s, Gibson saw teens intently hunched over video machines—and the idea of cyberspace hit him. Their eyes seemed frozen by this pale otherworldly light. Gibson turned the disturbing image into a novel, *Neuromancer*, the first novel to win science fiction's triple crown award. It became a cyberpunk classic, attracting a computer-savvy youth audience. According to Dewitt, "Critics were intrigued by a dense, technopoetic prose style that invites comparisons to Dashiell Hammett, William Burroughs and Thomas Pynchon. Computer-literate readers were drawn by Gibson's nightmarish depictions of an imaginary world disturbingly similar to the one they inhabit."[2]

In Gibson's fictional realm, cyberspace is a computer-generated landscape that characters enter by "jacking in"—sometimes by plugging electrodes directly into sockets implanted into the brain. What they see when they get there is a three-dimensional representation of all the information stored in "every computer in the human system"—great warehouses and skyscrapers of data.

In *Neuromancer* cyberspace is described as a place of "unthinkable complexity," with "lines of light ranged in the nonspace of the mind, clusters and constellations of data. Like city lights, receding."[3] This is an idealized vision of where cyberspace is heading.

At present, cyberspace teems with many millions of inhabitants all over the globe who send billions of signals across its electronic synapses. It includes, in the images of Dewitt, the rapidly expanding wireless services; microwave towers that carry great quantities of cellular phone and data traffic; communications satellites strung like beads in geosynchronous orbit; and low-flying satellites that will soon crisscross the globe like angry bees, connecting those who are too far-flung or too much on the go to be tethered by wires. Someday even our television sets may be part of cyberspace, transformed into interactive "teleputers" by so-called full-service networks like the ones several cable-TV companies (including Time Warner) are building along the old cable lines, using fiber optics and high-speed switches.

A Cornucopia of Information

What can cyberspace really do in its touted ability to transmit and navigate through oceans of information across the world?

In the spring of 1995 I traveled from Berkeley, California to the Cambridge University library in Cambridge, England, a trip that usually takes at least two days, using cars, planes, trains, and subways. I made the same trip by cyberspace, entering the same library in seconds through the Internet. The cyberspace visit cost pennies and was near instantaneous. The physical visit and flight to England cost far more (yet had different and tangible rewards). Of course there were differences. In the real world I parked behind the Cam River on the back side of Trinity College and wandered around the perimeter of Clare College to the library. Books could be held and retrieved, but this took time. In cyberspace, sifting through large numbers of books is much faster. Rather than writing a quotation on a note card in the stacks, scratching it out with pen or pencil, one can download (electronically transfer) the text "on-line" in a fraction of a second. Still, the Cambridge library—like our own Library of Congress—is far from getting all of its books in digital format, though the catalogs are digitized.

It is through the World Wide Web (WWW)—the most powerful and sophisticated of the Internet gateways—that it becomes simple and commonplace, for instance, to go from Berkeley to a town in Finland, to Rome, then Paris, *all in a matter of seconds*. This is called "surfing the Net." A work about Austrian poet Rainer Maria Rilke or French author Louis F. Céline at the Sorbonne can be found through cyberspace in far less time than crossing Paris on the Metro and working through the Sorbonne library system in person.

In cyberspace, a 100-page book, a color photograph of the Great Pyramid, or a small software program can be "downloaded" into a computer's memory in well under a minute (via a 28,800-baud Global Village Teleport Platinum modem connected to a Power Macintosh 8100 that has 32 megabytes of RAM, and a one gigabyte hard drive—yes, a new "computerese" language is emerging). That is the magic genie aspect of cyberspace—seemingly instantaneous access to knowledge in bit-streams of data that can lure you all over the world. (This is where less prepared minds can get trapped in cyberspace, as we will see later).

Yet this is only the beginning of the information explosion from the world's storehouse. A new interactive, indeed tactile, universe is emerging through cyberspace's most complex doorway—virtual reality. Rather than the still color images that most people get on the World Wide Web at the moment, one day a full immersion into a computer-generated alternate reality will be possible. What the mind thinks, reality will become. What is presently holding things up is that computers need much more data access to bring this off. Right now, the World Wide Web can only provide miniature "Quicktime" movies on a computer screen. But one day anyone will be able to put on a helmet and see wide spatial distances in full color in three dimensions—and maybe they won't need the helmet!

Perhaps the most powerful and immersive means of entering a virtual reality experience will not be by using a helmet, with its limited and crude screen and grainy pixel depth. Instead, it might be by means of a beam of cold laser light. This laser light will be beamed directly onto the retina. In that beam will be carried the full pixel depth of the outward world—50 million polygons a second—coming from a computer. (It has been alleged that in a high-secrecy military experiment, using the cold laser on the retina, a full 360 degree immersion took place and the subject experienced being in a simulated world that was as real as being in the real world.)

Then three-dimensional town meetings will take place, with levitating participants from around the world meeting in an electronic designer universe with any kind of backdrop conceivable. Although the participants may be in cities ranging from New Delhi to Bonn, they will be able to assemble together in a vast virtual space like Hindu gods gathering on some *Bardo* plane. Participants might decide to appear in designer-bodies—for instance, the CEO of a global database corporation "morphed" partway into an ancient Boddhisatva ("enlightened one") from Tibet meeting another software giant who is "morphed" into Zeus, and so forth. All of this lies in the near future as central processors—the brains behind computers (such as the Pentium and the Power PC)—become much more powerful, and as storage and transmission become truly immense. We are already partway there.

The Exponential Process

If a Power Macintosh RISC processor 604 alone has more power than 10,000 archaic Univac computers combined, what happens if millions of these RISC processors are connected? Few can sum up the vast scales of amplification that lie behind this new universe of digital power—utterly unknown in the 1940s—better than futurist George Gilder, a kind of dean of the technological edge. Gilder notes that we have seen the power of the computer chip not just in the individual case, but now interlinked as cells to a greater meta-chip. He gives the following example:

> The Emperor of China was totally infatuated with this new game of chess that had been invented for him. He was so grateful to the inventor that he came to him and said, "I'll give you anything you want in the kingdom as a tribute for this wonderful game you gave me."
>
> And the inventor said, "Well, I want one grain of rice. I want one grain of rice on the first square of the chess board, which has sixty-four squares, then I want two grains of rice on the second square. Four grains of rice on the third square, eight grains of rice on the fourth square and so on."

In other words, this is an exponential process.

And the Emperor happily granted this apparently modest request, and everything went fine for the first thirty-two squares. He could produce the several billion grains of rice fairly well on a quarter square mile of rice fields. But after the first thirty-two squares, things began to get interesting.

There are two ways the story ends. One is, the Emperor went bankrupt because after sixty-four squares, this was several billion trillion grains of rice, which would take the entire surface of the earth, plus the oceans times two to produce. The other end of the story was that the inventor lost his head.

But in any case, to get some perspective on how this applies, Kurzweil estimates that by 1993 there had been exactly thirty-two doublings of computer power since the first digital computers were invented in the early 1940s. So we've now completed the first half of the chess board, where things really become interesting and where the Emperor began to take notice of this process.[4]

Rather than grains of rice, Gilder tells us that microprocessors are on the chess board—increasing in quantity and power:

As we proceed into the second half of the chess board, as Ray puts it, the personal computer is just going to blow away television and all these broadcast technologies associated with it.

. . . Early in 1993, both Bill Gates and Andy Grove, the world's leading experts on computer production, essentially, both projected a great year. . . . Worldwide computer production in 1993 was nearly fifty million, almost 4 percent greater than most projections. This is a tremendous upside surprise.[5]

The fundamental particle of cyberspace is not the atom but the bit—the binary digit, a unit of data usually represented as a 0 or 1. Nicholas Negroponte, director of M.I.T.'s Media Lab, observes that information may still be delivered in magazines and newspapers (atoms), but the real value is in the contents (bits). Bits are different from atoms, Negroponte observes, and obey different laws. They are weightless. They are easily (and flawlessly) reproduced. There is an infinite supply. And they can be sent across cyberspace at nearly the speed of light. When it comes to moving bits across the earth in this new nervous system, barriers of time and space disappear.[6] Hence the Rilke passage from Paris to Berkeley is accomplished in mere minutes, reproduced on the screen and downloaded, all in digital form. Pictures can be made digital as well, whether it is a "home page" on the World Wide Web with graphics and pictures (scenes out of the movie *The Net*, for example), or NASA's Jupiter probe sending close-ups of Jupiter in streams of digital data back to earth to be assembled from the outer reaches of cyberspace. NASA bulletin boards in cyberspace carry the latest space shuttle photographs. Indeed, there are now declassified photos from several U.S. spy satellites available on the World Wide Web.

The Origins of Cyberspace

Thirty years ago, in "The Computers of Tomorrow" (*Atlantic*, May 1964), Martin Greenberger wrote about an earlier prediction of computers:

> Nineteen years ago, in July, 1945 . . . Vanneva Bush predicted that the "advanced arithmetical machines of the future" would be (a) electrical in nature, (b) far more versatile than accounting machines, (c) readily adapted for a wide variety of operations, (d) controlled by instructions, (e) exceedingly fast in complex computation, and (f) capable of recording results in reusable form.

This 1945 prediction has more than come true. Such machines are the basis of the Internet, which could not exist without them. How do such machines link together to create the Internet?

The Internet evolved from a computer system built 25 years ago by the Defense Department to enable academic and military researchers to continue to do government work, even if part of the network were taken out in a nuclear attack. It eventually linked universities, government facilities, and corporations around the world. They all shared the costs and technical work of running the system.[7]

Unlike most telephone transmissions, the Internet works on a "packet-switching" protocol. A packet-switching network is so decentralized that it is practically indestructible—which is the reason the Defense Department paid to create and expand the Internet, starting in the 1960s. Each message sent over the Internet is broken into its constituents—that is, into small units of data, or "packets." Each packet sent from your computer may take its own independent path to its destination, through different phone lines and connected computer networks. On arrival the packets, from a few to many hundreds, are reassembled into a complete message. This is a technical marvel, and it keeps the entire network as bottleneck-free as possible, since each packet follows a path that is, at the instant it departs, less crowded than all the others.[8]

The scientists who were given free Internet access in its early days quickly discovered that the network was good for more than official business. They used it to send each other private messages—electronic mail or e-mail—and to post news and information on public electronic bulletin boards known as USENET newsgroups. Over the years the Internet became a favorite haunt of graduate students and computer hackers, who loved nothing better than to stay up all night exploring its web-like connections and devising new and interesting things for people to do. They constructed elaborate fantasy worlds with Dungeons and Dragons themes. They built tools for navigating the Net—such as the University of Minnesota's "Gopher," which makes it easy for Internet explorers to tunnel from one place on the world network to another, and various other programs that can locate a particular word or program from vast libraries of data available to Net users. More and more newsgroups were added until the bulletin-board system had grown into a dense tangle of discussion topics with bizarre computer-coded titles, such as *alt.tasteless.jokes, rec.arts.erotica,* and *alt.barney.dinosaur.die.die.die.*[9]

Virtual Communities

What more than 30 million modem-equipped computer users around the world have discovered is that cyberspace allows them to leap over barriers of time, place, sex, and social status and connect with strangers who share a particular obsession or concern. "We're replacing the old drugstore soda fountain and town square, where community used to happen in the physical world," says Howard Rheingold, a Berkeley-based author who has written a book on what he calls "virtual communities."[10]

Along with Rheingold, the Bay area is full of cyberspace visionaries, from Jaron Lanier, inventor of the term "virtual reality," to the two main cyberspace magazines, *Wired,* based in San Francisco, and *Mondo 2000,* based in Berkeley. A large percentage of cyber-visionaries worldwide happen to live in Berkeley. Many have their own habitats not too far from the Spiritual Counterfeits Project (SCP). Inventive anarchy has always been in the air of Berkeley (which is why SCP remains in the belly of the beast). Berkeley also has a large population of computer wizards, hackers (programmers), and software gurus. The joke is that many of Berkeley's advanced hackers who barely know or talk to one another when they pass on the street probably gush with intimate confession once they meet anonymously over the Net—perhaps thinking the other person is in Norway rather than being a neighbor around the corner. (A gasp heard at Berkeley's Cafe Strada: "You mean you're the *Nirvanic Liberator?* And that's *Commander Cody?*)

There has never been anything like this. People can be totally vulnerable with utter strangers. They can also project various kinds of assumed identities into this new social realm, like folks at a perpetual *Beaux Arts* ball changing masks, accents, and stories while constantly moving through faceless crowds and encountering an unending stream of strangers behind changing masks. *You can be virtually anybody.*

But these virtual communities in cyberspace have quickly created rapidly expanding virtual red-light districts, ghettos of depravity, with meetings and deals being made. With an open gateway and no age limit, anyone can get in, as the cover of *Time* shows in its cyberporn issue. Curious young minds can see it all. It is far worse than a preteen walking down Hollywood Boulevard and seeing open displays of hard-core porn. This stuff is live and interactive, with predators on the loose reaching vulnerable young kids with names right out of *The Exorcist*: "Hi, Melinda, this is Captain Howdy." They might meet in kid cafes or one of countless conference rooms set up to discuss a range of topics.

This has created yet another social phenomenon—*cyberspace runaways*; not just kids leaving home, but this time kids being sent bus tickets by adults to rendezvous at secret locations. This is especially true among homosexual virtual ghettos. A "chicken hawk" on the Net can stake out some vulnerable lad with indeterminate sexual boundaries—another symptom of our permissive era with its broken families and open-mindedness about "alternative" lifestyles. Soon the child is recruited and initiated.

A 12-year-old boy flew from Seattle to San Francisco after being mailed a ticket by a gay pedophile. They met over the Internet. It probably went something like this: "Hello there Jeremy. This is Batman looking for Robin. I have a picture in your mailbox." Jeremy then downloads a hexadecimal GIF file [*alt.binary.erotica.pedophilia*], watches it through a graphical interface, and ends up blanching like the kid on the cover of *Time.* It might be a scene of sodomy or something worse, a shot of a San Francisco gay bathhouse in full swing ("anal justice," "rimming," and so forth). Jeremy can then be instructed to go to various global bulletin boards that carry thousands of pictures that would not be allowed even in the most hard-core adult stores in America. The stuff from Amsterdam and

Copenhagen is especially bad. It's all available: bestiality, bondage, sadomasochism, and kid porn. Jeremy's life suddenly takes a new turn, and he may never recover. *He is defiled.*

Time's cyberporn issue (June 26, 1995) gives one of many examples:

> Ten-year-old Anders Urmacher, a student at the Dalton School in New York City who likes to hang out with other kids in the Treehouse chat room on America Online, got E-mail from a stranger that contained a mysterious file with instructions for how to download it. He followed the instructions, and then he called his mom. When Linda Mann-Urmacher opened the file, the computer screen filled with 10 thumbnail-size pictures showing couples engaged in various acts of sodomy, heterosexual intercourse and lesbian sex. "I was not aware that this stuff was online," says a shocked Mann-Urmacher. "Children should not be subjected to these images."[11]

How available is cyberporn? Martin Rimm, a Carnegie Mellon research associate working on a study of pornography in cyberspace, discovered the answer. He used Carnegie Mellon computers to download 917,000 dirty pictures that ranged "from simple nudity to pictures of men and women having sex with animals. He tracked how often the pictures had been downloaded, or called up by a computer user—6.4 million times."[12] And that is not all that is on the Internet, not by a long shot.

The world's galleries in cyberspace bustle with activity like Manhattan on a Saturday night, with everybody up and partying. It seems a perfect cure for loneliness. Singles can meet over the Net. Or, you can surf through the various conference rooms, clubhouses, and gatherings and end up in the strangest places. A curious teen can plug into a bulletin board called "alt.witchcraft" and attend a virtual coven. He can also find out where a live coven meets in his geographical locale. It is an instant connection, a sort of Manhattan transfer, from gallery to gallery. Those who want to check out satanism, discover where to buy the drug "ecstasy," or find out where the next all-night

Rave concert is in Menlo Park can do it. This push to explore the Net is partly driven by the fact that everybody is faceless, anonymous. Like the Billy Idol song, the participants are "eyes without a face" and remain truly anonymous until they decide to meet in the flesh.

While anonymous intimacy grows on the Internet, friends and intimates in the *real* world are often put on hold as a new sort of addiction grows among those who have tasted the Internet. Irwin Winkler, who produced the movie *The Net*, which is among a new wave of cyberspace intrigue films released in the summer of 1995 (others are *Virtuosity* and *Johnny Mnemonic*), now describes himself as an "Internet widower." He says his wife has been disappearing for long hours on the Net. Once greeted cheerfully with martini and meal prepared, Winkler is now all but ignored by his wife when he comes through the door. His wife stares transfixed at a computer screen, while navigating the World Wide Web, barely acknowledging his presence.

Governing Anarchy

Computer wizards subscribe to a somewhat anarchistic ethic, stated most succinctly in Steven Levy's *Hackers*. Among its tenets are: 1) Access to computers should be unlimited and total. 2) All information should be free. (This is where software piracy comes in; one student at M.I.T. posted copyrighted software, giving away millions of dollars of it before he was busted.) 3) Mistrust authority. 4) Promote decentralization.

This "ethic" has the feel of a 60s cliché. Nevertheless, the Internet was built up by people who lived and breathed this hacker ethic—students at Berkeley and M.I.T., researchers at AT&T Bell Laboratories, and computer designers at companies such as Apple and Sun Microsystems. "If there is a soul of the Internet, it is in that community," says Mark Stahlman, president of New Media Associates, a research firm in New York City.

Originally a relatively small community, the Internet could be self-policing. Anybody who got out of line was shouted down or shunned. But now that the population of the Net is larger than most European countries, those informal rules of behavior are starting to break down. "The Internet is becoming Balkanized, and where the mainstream culture and hacker culture clash, open battles are breaking out."[13]

One area of contention is the commercialization of the Net. There are also arguments over taste, ethics, and "netiquette." New usurpers on the Internet are disdained even more. A good example is found in two lawyers from Phoenix, Laurence Canter and Martha Siegel, who advertised their wares on the Internet (getting aliens green cards for the right fee) by "spamming"—a way of mass-posting information to tens of thousands of global bulletin boards. In response, the two lawyers were "flamed" by vast numbers of angry Internet fire ants who found interesting ways of punishing them; reportedly bombarding their Internet mailbox till the regional system overloaded, locking up their hard drive, sending computer viruses downstream hidden in responses, getting their fax machine to spew out reams of paper, sending them hideous messages, and so forth. One Norwegian hacker devised a program that would hunt for their messages on the Net and destroy them. (Keep in mind that most gifted hackers are on the far right of the bell-shaped curve.)

Also keep in mind that significant damage can be done by gifted hackers in cyberspace. On-line crimes include illegally transferring electronic funds, debiting visa cards and bank accounts (major banks report that millions are being stolen every day this way), raiding the Pentagon computer and stealing defense secrets, messing up flight schedules of commercial airlines, confusing air traffic controllers, changing college grade point averages in university central computers, and the like. Many in the media are alleging these and more serious "terrorist" crimes, indicating a real need for greater policing of the Net.

An early cyberspace film entitled *War Games*, starring Matthew Broderick, was based on a young whiz kid who used his home computer to electronically tap into the North American Air Defense Command (NORAD), then tricked the defense computer into "believing" (we are forced into using terms that apply to human cognition) that a nuclear confrontation was taking place between America and the former Soviet Union. Things escalated quickly, once the computer's codes were set in motion, to the brink of nuclear war. A vast arsenal of missile silos opened, with jet engines beginning to whine. Only a computer genius could reverse the process. With seconds left in the countdown, the earth was spared. But the movie message is clear regarding the threat of computer-savvy minds entering into forbidden places. The plot was not solely fiction.

Computer hackers have already penetrated NORAD, the Pentagon computer, the Central Intelligence Agency's Langley complex, and many other security-tight computers in the public sector. On the other side, the military is dreaming up new ways to engage in cyber-warfare. Military hackers could disable phone systems, commerce, airport control towers, defense computers, and so forth. There have been rumors about the CIA's advanced hackers transferring funds from Swiss bank accounts of political enemies. Fiction author Tom Clancy has written about such things.

Clifford Stoll, a University of California (Berkeley) physics faculty member and BMUG (Berkeley Macintosh User Group) hacker, discovered that an East German spy ring had gotten into a number of America's defense computers via the Internet. (I was at the BMUG meeting where Stoll told his story.) The hacker jumped from computer to computer, figuring out passwords and hiding out inside each one. Then onward he would go, camouflaging behind names the computer knew. Stoll's slightly fictionalized account of finding the cyber-spy ring, entitled *The Cuckoo's Egg*, was on the *New York Times* bestseller list. Stoll has also unmasked the darker side of cyberspace—its depersonalization and perversity—in his book *Silicon Snake Oil.* Related to this, Stoll remarked in an interview, "People don't like it when you spit at the god's eye, especially when they think you're one of them."[14]

Dreams of Godhood

The idealized utopian hope of cyberspace is that it might enable the human mind to be amplified by machine in the same way that machines, from bulldozers to jets, amplify human physical abilities. An athlete who can run only 20 miles per hour can move thousands of miles per hour in a supersonic jet. Bulldozers and cranes enable people to lift tens of thousands of pounds, far beyond their natural abilities. No one really knows where the cyberspace phenomenon is going. But at its root is human consciousness operating the machine. What will happen to human consciousness during this strange marriage is the issue at stake.

Some anticipate that cyberspace will become a true planetary nervous system, an electronic ocean of digital consciousness, where human minds enhanced by computer technology form a godlike alliance. They hope a global mind will appear through this and bring to fruition Marshal McLuhan's metaphor (McLuhan, a Canadian academic and author of *The Medium Is the Message,* coined the term "global village.") It will be a dream come true for those who believe in the awakening consciousness of the earth into the goddess, Gaia. Others look to the vaunted paradigm shift of the cosmic millennium. But it could equally become the new tower of Babel—bringing unity to the world electronically—and a doorway into techno-tyranny. It is by no means inconsistent that it could be both at the same time. A utopia for one can be a hell-on-earth for another. The two are not mutually exclusive.

A Darker Future

A perfect example of the dark side of cyberspace appeared almost 50 years ago in a futuristic novel. George Orwell's literary classic *1984* introduced the concept of a two-way television that looked back at the viewer. It was interactive and would constantly monitor everything that happened in the private dwelling of every viewer. Anyone whispering or conspiring, or who looked circumstantially guilty of "thought crimes," had only moments between the suspicious event "seen" by the TV and the arrival of State police in full force.

Winston, the main character in *1984*, was utterly diminished by the two-way television overlooking his room. He was forced to duck around a slim section of wall out of its view to find his diary hidden behind a loose brick. He was permitted no solitude and had to scrounge for brief interludes of privacy. If he was out of view for more than a few seconds—one of his few remaining strands of liberty—the screen would bark at him. If the techno-eye of Big Brother was not satisfied with his response, he knew it could order storm troopers. It would begin with threats, such as when he refused to do his morning calisthenics. Winston was reduced to a number, a mere cog in the State machine. In the end, another monitoring device reported him to the central system, and he was sent to be brainwashed. Winston the individual was erased. There was no room for an independent mind in the collective State, which needed intrusive and interactive ways of monitoring its human fold behind every wall.

Such a device exists today. In fact, it resembles the two-way TV in *1984*. It is merely the Orwellian application that is lacking. For now, you can order pizza or tickets to a sporting event if you are in Europe. But there are ways, "for the good of the many," to bring in-house monitoring on a mass scale— for example, to keep intruders from breaking into your house. Other crimes can be "seen" as well. If the TV sees an "ecological" crime, such as pouring solvent down a drain, in comes the State apparatus. Not police at first. Perhaps, rather, notification of a fine is sent in the mail or debited from the offender's account. In time, more and more parameters of an individual's life would be under observation—again, for the good of the many.

Singapore has already embarked on this course. Today it could be described as a "benign techno-dictatorship." Singapore's proposed National Information Infrastructure (NII)—which aims to wire up every home by the year 2005 with optical fibers of almost unlimited carrying capacity—offers various attractive options from this new technology. Patients will be able to stay at home while linked to the hospital by a bedside terminal that monitors their progress and transmits the results. Dynamic road signs will automatically warn drivers of conditions ahead. Bus stops will display the expected arrival time of the next bus. The NII will also be used for watching sporting events around the world, viewing the treasures of the Louvre or the Smithsonian Institution, playing long-distance interactive computer games, and downloading video rentals.[15] Of course, it could be used to watch other things as well—*its own citizens.* The techno-eye can go both ways. And it has in Singapore.

In what the media call "another of Singapore's experiments in social engineering," taxis are soon to be monitored by satellite. "Cablink" will ensure that taxis work to maximum efficiency with minimum cruising time. (If this works it can be extended to all automobiles, and why not?) Already taxis are outfitted with alarms that activate when they exceed 80 kilometers per hour. Of real concern, however, is the thought that Singapore is trial-testing a system destined for the industrial nations of the West during the promised era of the world order. Some social planners really do think that far ahead, as does Singapore's Oxford-educated leader.

Aldous Huxley's *Brave New World* portrayed a different type of techno-dictatorship than Orwell's. It was less austere and less blatantly cruel. It used the pleasure principle rather than punishment as the prime motivator of the docile masses. The citizens were manipulated through controlled economy and entertainment, "bread and circuses." If Singapore embodies the Orwellian approach as far as rules and punishment and disdain of the corrupting influence of the pleasure principle are concerned, the West could head—indeed *is* heading—in the Huxleyan direction, through permissiveness (a perverse redefinition of real freedom), pleasure, and guaranteed welfare.

A Ghost in the Machine

Consider this haunting image: It is a rock concert of the future, perhaps around the year 2000. An audience of more than 100,000 people are on custom "dental-style" reclining chairs in a vast underground stadium that has been laser-melted. Concertgoers can look out at a broad expanse where they can see the rock band live if they choose not to use special viewing goggles. Within the vaster expanse above the band, holographic images of gigantic proportions are projected in empty space. The audience is fed designer drugs of choice through tubes. They are also wired to body-sensation devices incorporating what we would now call virtual reality headgear. The sound system is incredible—fully digital. Rock music, designer drugs, and electronics, all for the total experience that completely overwhelms the individual.

The concert's underground laser-melted arena is a kind of replica of the human lung. Just over the coliseum, a giant metallic-grey command tower rises above ground, surrounded by a landscaped rustic wilderness. The only clues to the underground auditorium are the modern subway-style escalators that emerge at tunnel entrances away from the tower. The tower harbors the technological engines that run the rock concert. Vast cables go in and out of it. The tower also performs another function, of which the audience is oblivious. It probes concertgoers through brain-body sensors in their hi-tech body gear and can look back *into their minds.*

Now the image takes a strange turn. Powerful entertainment moguls in the tower, far from public view, surround a supercomputer that is far beyond the CRAY computer (one of the world's fastest, most powerful computers). What is of terrible concern is that a massive spiritual force—a demonic presence—is mind-melding with the computer that is the interlink between the human controllers and the audience. In the digital feed of rock lyrics, the words are being interpolated on a higher level and somehow carry morpheme and phoneme messages to the inner minds of the listeners. They are being invaded with some deeper message. Beneath the entertainment are behavior and personality modification. The audience of mostly youth have become clay in the hands of the triumvirate of powers in the grey tower. Distracted by pleasure, defeated in spirit, they are being prepared for something other than entertainment. In a strange way, they are being domesticated. Perhaps, in the days of Babylon, we would say enchanted.

The above image was a visionary awake-dream I had in Costa Brava, Spain, months before going to India where I spent several years with an Indian power yogi. It took place at the exact time of the Woodstock concert in America. I learned this two days after the dream when I saw the cover of *Time* magazine. I felt a strange kind of shock when I read about this concert in upstate New York, with half a million or so of my generation. Far from an ordinary dream, I remembered every detail. It will be curious to see how far it approximates real history.[16]

A Giant Digital Ganges

During the mid-1980s, when Mitch Kapor and Bill Gates were America's young software prodigies, Kapor named his software company Lotus—simple, elegant, and quietly reflective of his spiritual leanings. The lotus is the flower upon which the Hindu god Vishnu reclines as "preserver of the cosmos." In real life, Kapor's Lotus 1-2-3 is a powerful spreadsheet program that has become something of an industry standard. (Meanwhile, Gates founded Microsoft, a global corporate empire.) In 1990 Kapor and Grateful Dead lyricist John Barlow started the Electronic Frontier Foundation to defend the civil liberties of hackers in cyberspace. They also shared a similar worldview common in cyberspace.

Robert Wright of *Wired* magazine makes this observation about Kapor and Barlow:

> Kapor is being true to hacker culture, which exudes a nearly mystical faith in the benign force of uninhibited information. Barlow often cites Pierre Teilhard de Chardin, the Jesuit priest who envisioned the technological assembly of a planetary "noosphere," a global brain that would seal humanity's spiritual destiny: Point Omega. "Whether or not it represents Teilhard's vision," he has written, "it seems clear we are about some Great Work here—the physical wiring of collective human consciousness. The idea of connecting every mind to every other mind in full-duplex broadband is one which, for a hippie mystic like me, has clear theological implications."[17]

Cyberspace, by its very unitive structure, tends toward a functional pantheism. Besides that, the reigning beliefs of cyber-culture are post-Christian, globalistic, and unitive. It is a demographic of the young, privileged, and bright who are demonstrably post-Christian. To them, this electronic plane functions like a giant digital Ganges—unifying people, nations, thoughts, and concepts almost mystically.

India's great river is its living symbol of an ancient belief— Hindu, Advaitist, Vedantist, monist, Yogic—that all things are one and that all things return to the final source, *the One*, from which they are said to come. The Ganges is India's natural symbol—its living metaphor—of this process. For this ancient river is seen as the collector of lesser rivers and tributaries, and the body into which all things flow and join. It becomes in some ways the great repository of Indian civilization down through the millennia. Pantheism, by its very nature, finds unity at the lowest common denominator, at the base of existence. Unity, to the Eastern mystical mind, is the great center of existence. But for those who see Hinduism up close (such as myself, having once converted to it) this unity comes at a terrible price, for it is built upon the oldest spiritual lie—that we shall be as God. The Ganges, upon closer inspection, is able to unify, but only on a baser level.

To one pilgrim from the West, this unity at the bottom of the universe is also visually evident in the ebb and flow of the Ganges river, which he describes with rare lucidity:

> We reach the Ganges and take a boat ride. All the buildings we can see from the river are in various stages of dilapidation. The heat and the moisture have eaten into stone, brick, and plaster; everything is pockmarked, with that leprous aspect that over-takes even decently constructed buildings when, in tropical lands, nobody cares and everything decays.
>
> On the steps leading down to the river and on the stone land-ings are masses of people. Pilgrims and locals doing their . . . well, what should one call it?—acts of private life. The dirty green river becomes bathroom, toilet, mouthwash, laundromat, drinking place for animal and man. Fully or half-immersed, people wash their hair, their underwear, rinse their mouths, and defecate, as the freely floating dung testifies. All this with the utmost matter-of factness, without embarrassment. Our oarsman, sweating under the beating sun, leans over the side and slurps palms-full of water.
>
> On this horrifying boat ride, I no longer know whether we are navigating the River Styx or gliding with Dante in a liquid hell. We come in sight of the funeral pyres. On the way to Benares we had passed trucks loaded with white wrapped bodies, corpses brought by families from distant villages. All day the pyres burn, and every three hours or so a white or red-clad, garlanded, cadaver is laid on top. There it burns for hours.
>
> . . . What attracts and keeps them here is the degradation: of reason, of self esteem, of vital forces, of faith in God and man. Here they find innumerable gods and none at all; everybody may do his thing just like the monkeys and the cows, sinking slowly toward the Ganges or Nirvana. Intelligence and purpose-fulness dissolve on the trashheap, the body rots until it becomes one with the road, the grass, the dung. The great nothingness envelops all, and the ashes go into the river.[18]

Cyberspace, in some ways, reminds me of a giant digital Ganges. Like the timeless river crossing India, it promises to unify. And no doubt it will create the appearance of unity as it flows along the digital plane, but perhaps at a great price—by absorbing the lowest elements of human nature, that substrate of human desire and experience that occupies an expanse of darkness. Like the Ganges, where things decompose then converge back, so too with the digital plane. Unity will come through a convergence of substrates—and that is one of the most ancient themes of the occult, its dark secret where unity and power meet at the bottom. We will look into this theme at varying times throughout this book.

2

WELCOME TO THE CYBER-MILLENNIUM

Donald L. Baker

---------------- OVERVIEW ----------------

As we approach the twenty-first century, change is accelerating rapidly due to the unique interplay between the technology that has created cyberspace and the changing worldview of the West. The West is suddenly crossing over from Modernism to Postmodernism, ending Modernism's several-hundred-year reign. If the result of all this is a new sort of cyber-millennium by the twenty-first century, will this new social order be driven by such forces as global economics and entertainment, or forces much deeper? This chapter calls it a "high-stakes battleground in an amoral and postmodern society." Will the new cyber-millennium keep out the knowledge of God, like some new despotic Roman emperor, or will there be new entranceways into this vast global network through which its inhabitants can be reached? Such issues are vital right now.

We are entering an era of electronically extended bodies living at the intersection points of the physical and virtual worlds, of occupation and interaction through telepresence as well as through physical presence, . . . and of new, soft cities that parallel, complement, and sometimes compete with our existing urban concentrations of brick, concrete, and steel.[1]

–William J. Mitchell, *City of Bits*

T he great work[2] of the cyber (third) millennium—networking the world for digital cyberspace—is underway. The governments of the United States, Western Europe, Japan, and China are pushing it; businesses are hoping to make money through on-line commerce and on-line banking; cyber-savvy Americans are snapping up computer hardware and software for home use, while the kids are accessing CD-ROMs and Internet-based resources at school. Brick by digital brick, the city of bits is being erected before our eyes.

41

People still ask whether it's inevitable? In a word: *yes*. The acceleration of worldwide digitization and networking is approaching escape velocity, pulling free from the material world into cyberspace. Nothing will deter our society's trajectory into the electronic ether. The recent expansion of world markets has made competition and communication only more intense. There will be fits and starts, missed deadlines, and the inevitable glitches inherent in software development. But the final result is virtually inescapable; it is in many senses already here.

CyberWhat?

The cyber-millennium dawned in 1989[3] in the wake of the fall of European communism with its dogma of centralized social and economic planning. In the post-postwar New World Order, Asian communist nations—China, Vietnam, and North Korea—are tottering. Their obsolete authoritarian structures will, the cyberphiles* say, eventually collapse as their citizens enter the decentralizing city of bits. *And enter they must.* The world's nations know they must upgrade their telecommunications networks lest they be left behind in the datacloud.[4]

Crossing into the cyber-millennium, we have left the 20th century and with it, Modernity. We remember Modernity, vaguely—the Enlightenment project founded on the replacement of Christendom with a utopia of humanity redeemed and transformed by reason and science alone. With the failure of overweening Modernity and the arrival of postmodernism, we have reached the moment (to borrow H. G. Wells's phrase) of the "mind at the end of its tether."

A Word About Postmodernism

Postmoderism was for several years the playground of art historians, philosophers, and professor-novelists who noted the shift in Cold War culture away from modernist faith—

---

*Cyberspace enthusiasts.

democratic and Marxist—in the absolute truth of progress through reason and science. The failures of Modernity (for example, The Somme, Auschwitz, Prague 1968, Brasilia, *Challenger,* Bhopal, Gorbachev) confounded atheist academics, who began first to believe and then teach that with God "dead" and Modernity fatally flawed, why not ditch the lot, and believe all facts, all reality, to be relative and social constructions. The postmodernist result, notes Gene Edward Veith, is that "intellect is replaced by the will. Reason is replaced by emotion. Morality is replaced by relativism. Reality itself becomes a social construct."[5] Suspicion that something is not right becomes pervasive. Recent generations, tutored by their professors, rejected not only Modernity but the entire Western heritage propagated by those infamous dead, white European males. The baby-boomers' sense of mission has ensured that these radical theories trickle-down to the elementary schools.[6]

It is no small matter that the technologies of cyberspace have arrived at precisely the same historical moment that communism has fallen to secular capitalism, and Western culture—even the United States—has rejected not only belief in God's active reality, but also the anti-Christian Enlightenment project. While Western corporations are busily establishing trade with former enemies and other rapidly developing nations, postmodernist theorists are teaching students to deconstruct the entire infrastructure of reason-based reality, and to replace it with a pastiche of multiculturalism, premodern (but non-Christian) religion, and new ideas about what it means to be human in an age of silicon-based machines.

Just as Renaissance Europeans projected their own hopes and fears as myths about the New World, various groups are struggling to establish and control the underlying myths of cyberspace. Of these groups, the post-Marxists are the greatest enemy of the kingdom of God. For while the capitalists will accommodate us (so long as they turn a profit on our business), and the personal-freedom zealots will defend our right to Net access (so long as we do not stuff Jesus down their throats in the *alt.sex.stories* newsgroup), the postmodern neo Marxists and their fellow travelers are overtly hostile not only to the gospel of Christ, but also to our personal and social practice of Christian morality.

Why? Because Christianity is anathema to postmodernists. It stubbornly proclaims a the reality of overarching truth: that there exists one true Father God (not mother goddess) who must be worshipped and obeyed (eliminating many alternative lifestyles), and who can be approached and known only through submission to Jesus (yet another male patriarchal figure).

Reaching the Millennial Generation

The colonization and definition of cyberspace is *not* primarily a leisure pursuit, but very much a conscious project of organizations and individuals who view cyberspace as a tool to advance toward particular goals. Since its origins, cyberspace has become indispensable as a medium for managing the increasing complexity and data necessary for business, science, and the military to function. The balance of cyberspace-related industry, however, has developed either 1) to make money providing new consumer products and diversions, or 2) to advance transformative social agendas. It is the second goal I will focus on here.

The cyberspace industry eagerly awaits the first cyber-generation. In a *Ministries Today* article, Michael Thompson describes the kids born from the 1980s to the year 2000. Three of nine "sociological shapers" that Thompson says distinguish this generation from baby-boomers and the so-called Generation-X concern their heavy involvement in electronic technologies (media saturation, technological advancement, and the global village). Thompson notes:

> The Millennial Generation is literally addicted to visual and audio media. . . . Fifty percent of these kids own an

answering machine or a CD player. Ninety percent own a stereo. Three out of 10 own their own personal computer. They are mesmerized by technological advancement.[7]

In the dawning cyber-millennium, efforts to make new disciples of Christ will soon shift from baby-boomers and Generation-Xers to include the millennial generation. Thompson says it is essential to understand this group in light of their affinity for electronic media. While F2F (netspeak for "face-to-face") will no doubt continue to be the most common mode for personal evangelism, an increasing amount of seed-sowing will be accomplished on-line, in electronic agoras and on digital Mars Hills. This is why we should know something of the hidden building blocks of cyberspace.

City of Bits: Frontier Town?

In 1990, gentleman rancher, Grateful Dead lyricist, and Internet enthusiast John Perry Barlow wrote:

> Cyberspace, in its present condition, has a lot in common with the 19th century West. It is vast, unmapped, culturally and legally ambiguous . . . hard to get around in, and up for grabs. Large institutions already claim to own the place, but most of the actual natives are solitary and independent, sometimes to the point of sociopathy. It is, of course, a perfect breeding ground for both outlaws and new ideas about liberty.[8]

Later that same year, in a manifesto announcing their creation of the Electronic Frontier Foundation (EFF), Barlow and Lotus 1-2-3 inventor Mitchell Kapor called cyberspace

> a frontier region, populated by the few hardy technologists who can tolerate the austerity of its savage computer interfaces, incompatible communications protocols, proprietary barricades, cultural and legal ambiguities, and general lack of useful maps or metaphors.[9]

In the mid-1990s, cyberspace is still "up for grabs." But little else of Barlow and Kapor's description has remained unchanged. The Internet, once the government-supported research and communications domain of university and military researchers, now supports an estimated 50 million users worldwide, with thousands of "newbies" coming on-line every day. The two leading on-line service providers, America Online and CompuServe, have linked their private networks to the Internet and now claim more than 12 million subscribers together. Software behemoth Microsoft is joining the fray with its own on-line service linked to Windows 95. New software tools such as Yahoo and Netscape have made it much easier to navigate and publish on the Net.

But is cyberspace really being settled like a frontier region from the Old West? No—not if one examines the historical record. Most Western settlement was accomplished not by isolated individuals "lighting out for the territory" like Huckleberry Finn, but by families and communities who built towns and neighboring farms. Settlers were usually not solitary, independent, or "sociopathic" outlaws, but *conservative* folk hoping to reproduce the culture of the towns they had left behind. "Colonization by congregation and kinship groups . . . refutes the argument that the pioneers were champions of 'individualism,'" notes historian Page Smith. "The lonely, wide-ranging frontiersmen bulk large in historical fiction and in the popular mind, but they counted for little in comparison with the town-builders of the covenant."[10]

In truth, cyberspace more closely resembles the 19th century *urban* West—mapped and promoted by profit-seeking investors (America Online, electronic shopping centers), and settled primarily not by individuals but by corporate and academic communities. Many settlers—particularly on the Internet—behave as inhabitants of a postmodern urban landscape (which, of course, most of them are in real life). The Internet in particular is an unzoned megalopolis where pornographers hawk their wares across the street from schools and meeting halls, and wild-eyed anarchists distribute electronic pamphlets alongside the new CommerceNet shopping center. In seconds, a World Wide Web surfer can double-click from "Thomas," the Library of Congress home page, to the *Hustler* magazine site—and much worse.

Why, then, did Barlow and Kapor deliberately engage the attractive imagery of the frontier in describing cyberspace? Perhaps it was because their inaccurate reading of history was a good fit for the Electronic Frontier Foundation, which helps channel political debate of cyberspace toward guaranteeing the greatest amount of legal protection for cybernauts' file transfers and personal communications. This agenda includes drafting laws, or amending old ones, to eliminate legal gray areas when adapting traditional business practices and the Bill of Rights to the city of bits.

Barlow and Kapor's choice of "hot-button" Old West imagery to describe cyberspace to the TV generation was a shrewd, largely successful attempt to garner support for their free-speech agenda. They devised "a mythical history and an impossible origin in emptiness,"[11] while soft-pedaling what many netizens (Internet citizens) had half-forgotten: the Internet's roots as a U.S. Government-funded, defense-related computer network used by thousands of workers in the Cold War military-industrial-educational complex.[12] The frontier (or "backward-looking") model of cyberspace is aimed at those netizens to whom on-line access and activity are rights to be protected and expanded, not controlled by government.

While Barlow admits, "I certainly don't claim we're creating a [cyberspace] utopia,"[13] other netizens do. The following manifesto, penned by one S. Boxx of Denver, Colorado, is typical of the genre:

> The ideology of "electronic democracy" [electracy] is that a vast cyberspatial revolution and renaissance is in progress at the very moment, stealthily bubbling beneath our noses. While it appears that there is no orderly progress taking place on the Internet, it is actually brimming with vast

forces of creativity and ingenuity. These forces are almost
about to be unleashed in an unprecedented explosion of
light and heat. . . . Today only a few isolated visionaries are
aware of the vast, untapped force of this lumbering, slum-
bering giant. But soon the Savior of Cyberspace will be
making his appearance. . . . [14]

Some of these screeds are indeed "brimming with vast
forces of creativity and ingenuity," thereby inviting further
interchange (mostly the abuse known as a "flame"*) concerning their total loopiness. One cannot have a postmodern
city, however, without a Hyde Park (or, I would argue, a Mars
Hill)—and it is good for us that the city of bits has any
number of such places, and their defenders.

. . . Or Locus of Control?

As cyberspace becomes an essential workplace for more
people worldwide, its reality as a *city*—not a frontier or village—of bits becomes more evident. The complexity of transactions and communications drives the need for more market
and storage space. Growing risks from muggers (computer
hackers), vandals (computer viruses), and perverts (on-line
creeps) spawns a growing need for order and control. This
city model promotes cyberspace as a realm created to store,
control, and manipulate the overload of data. In this forward-
looking model, the focus is on creating rather than discov-
ering an electronic realm; on its use primarily by government
and business rather than by individuals; and on data manipulation and control rather than personal freedom. This cyberspace model favors regulating and restricting on-line
communications and uploaded content, rather than the frontier model's freedom to communicate with anyone desired
and to access and download any type of on-line file. Calls for
the regulation or elimination of on-line smut (how can such

---

*A hostile, nasty electronic message sent via e-mail.

regulations succeed in a worldwide network of the unre-
deemed?) assume this model of cyberspace.

The backward-looking frontier model attracts the free-
speech utopians, while this forward-looking city model
attracts those who believe that on-line data-sifting and manipulation will somehow produce knowledge and wisdom. The
trend today is not to teach children facts—which in postmodern society are suspect anyway—but instead to train them
in information retrieval and sorting. Derrick de Kerckhove,
director of the University of Toronto's McLuhan Program,
puts it this way:

> Why bother learning all this stuff yourself if you have access
> to it when you need it? Quite the reverse, you might find
> value in not knowing something, as the very process of dis-
> covering anything may be more useful and exciting than the
> content of the discovery. With real expert systems, improved
> by sophisticated neural networks with rapid learning curves,
> you don't need to be an expert in anything.[15]

You don't need to be a learner at all, I suppose. Just the
ticket for kids who cannot place the Civil War in the 19th century! The assumption is that if those of the millennial generation are trained in data manipulation rather than stuffing
their heads with useless old facts and other lessons from
human experience, they will somehow be able to make sense
of retrieved on-line information. Langdon Winner calls this
wrongheaded belief "mythinformation," and points out:

> What is the "information" so cherished as knowledge? It is
> not understanding, enlightenment, critical thought, time-
> less wisdom, or the content of a well-educated mind.
> Looking closely at the writings of computer enthusiasts,
> "information" means enormous quantities of data manipu-
> lated by various kinds of electronic media. . . . [16]

If students have no underlying factual structures and
value systems through which to contextualize and evaluate

newly acquired information, how can they possibly ascend the slope that leads from unorganized information to synthesized knowledge, and finally to clearheaded wisdom? Cyberspace technologies will not help the millennial generation extract knowledge and wisdom from data if they are not *taught* to recognize that some ideas are more important than others and some are, in fact, true and worth emulating. Internalizing the teachings of the Bible, for example, will be far more useful for life than any number of database "hits" without context or underlying values. What is needed in the cyber-millennium, Michael Novak believes, is to

> learn again how to teach the virtues of the noble Greeks and Romans, the commandments God entrusted to the Hebrews, and the virtues that Jesus introduced into the world—even into secular consciences—such as gentleness, kindness, compassion, and the equality of all in our Father's love. We must celebrate again the heroes, great and humble, who have for centuries exemplified the virtues proper to our individual peoples. We must learn again how to speak of virtue, character, and nobility of soul.[17]

The huge sales of William Bennett's *Book of Virtues* show that many people agree.

While the early cyber-millennium on-line culture is heavily tilted toward the frontier free-speech model, the control concept may ultimately win out—to our dismay. That is because the Net and future interactive-TV networks are forecast to become home to a multibillion-dollar cybermall—once enough people are enticed to peel off crisp new, digital e-dollars*[18] for products hawked on-line. Behind all the buying, selling, and market research hides an inescapable reality: *datamining.* Commercial on-line services regularly vacuum data on customers' on-line habits; software companies are feverishly developing programs to direct sophisticated metering of

---

*Electronic dollars.

"hits" at corporate Web sites. And do not forget all your ATM visits and credit card purchases—those are stored in cyber-space, too. Urban planner Michael Sorkin notes,

> It is an irony . . . that in many ways the most enfranchised members of the electronic city are those willing to submit to the most draconian forms of observation. To fully partici-pate in the electronic city is to have virtually all of one's activities recorded, correlated and made available to an enormous invisible government of credit agencies, back office computer banks and endless media connections. To exist in the public realm means to be wired in. The ultimate consequence is that the body, the person, no longer simply exists in public space but actually becomes it. . . . The media system—the electronic city—is all about the disappearance of privacy, about the surrender of all aspects of personhood to visibility and manipulation.[19]

Knowing Revelation 13 by heart is not necessary for Sorkin's insight to generate a primal, fight-or-flight response. How ironic that the frontier model, with its exciting lure of freedom and privacy, migrates the masses not to empty cyber-space vistas, but to data-crowded virtual cities where—as urban cyber-consumers—we willingly submit to ever-greater surveillance and control.

Data Kills, But the Spirit Gives Life

"Data kills, but the Spirit gives life."

That is what Vancouver School of Theology professor, David Lochhead, says. He explains:

> Information that is given its value and purpose by enabling the exploitation, the manipulation, the alienation of human beings is demonic. Information technology does have the power to exploit and oppress. But it also has the power to heal. . . . The technology of bits and bytes can become a medium of the Spirit. It can be a means by which

we reach out and touch our neighbor and, in that touch, a word of faith, of reconciliation, of hope, is spoken.[20]

I quote Lochhead because, like him, I am ultimately hopeful about the church's potential to spread the knowledge and grace of God in the city of bits. I have written above on the two dominant models of cyberspace because techno-hype obscures the reality: cyberspace is becoming a high-value, high-stakes battleground in an amoral, postmodern society. Many of us are already working and playing in cyberspace, without thinking much about the hidden political and economic dynamics influencing the space behind our screens. The millennial generation will have little choice—from childhood, they will log-on, jack-in, and Net-surf. Unless we wish to join the Amish in principled cultural irrelevancy, we will stop fearing cyberspace, and learn where it is going in the cyber-millennium.

Then we will go there, too. We will teach our kids the value of books over video, the Bible over Beavis, and F2F ("face to face") over virtual relationships. We will also ask God to guide us in:

- making sure our kids are computer-savvy, while not becoming addicted;

- monitoring their use of software and their on-line friendships;

- making positive contributions to selected conference forums, newsgroups, and mailing lists;

- developing personal e-mail relationships with selected Christians and unbelievers;

- contributing to on-line e-journals* and archives, or starting our own;

---

*Electronic journals.

- helping create "Mars Hill" situations for gospel presentations in live forums on America Online, CompuServe, and other commercial services;

- creating Web pages with either heavy (evangelistic) or light (pre-evangelistic) Christian content;

- providing hypertext links on our Web pages to good-quality Christian and secular Web sites;

- encouraging our churches and parachurch ministries to set up their own Web sites;

- joining the privacy advocates in negotiating privacy guarantees for on-line purchases and other personal data;

- contributing letters to the editors of *Wired* and other influential cyber-culture journals.

Those of faith will need to navigate the city of bits with dexterity and caution that Christians have had to show down the ages during hostile times—from ancient Rome to modern New York—remaining in but not always "of" the world. The digital environment offers perils and temptations that a modern-day John Bunyan might well describe in a digital *Pilgrim's Progress Through Cyberspace*. Yet it is also a time of acute need, when wanderers on the electronic plane become easily lost since they have no ultimate road-map of meaning. Such people can—and must—be reached.

3

VIRTUAL
MAN

John Moore

───────────── OVERVIEW ─────────────

Will human nature take a much anticipated "evolutionary leap" through cyberspace technology? Some futurists speculate that an anticipated quantum leap will come through untapped potentials unleashed deep in the recesses of the human mind. Others are looking into the potentials of cyber-technology as a passage to a kind of virtual immortality. They ponder the question of whether it is possible to download a human mind into a big enough computer to store it forever with personality intact. Of course, such humanists never question whether a spirit or soul could ever be part of the human makeup. Could all of these attempts at techno-enhancement backfire, creating a kind of cyber-Frankenstein? John Moore explores some of these frontline issues.

The process . . . [of "downloading" a human mind into a computer] involves precise mapping, copying, and simulating in a neural net computer every structure and pattern in the human brain. The consciousness those biological structures and patterns supported should then reboot, reanimate as a separate, evolving cyberspace intelligence . . . I propose that this moment be known as your bootday.

—Professor Mel Seesholtz,
Pennsylvania State University[1]

I read the article in which the above quotation appears. Then I reread it. Then I went back to read it through for a third time. My sense of amazement grew with each reading. The ideas were not new to me. My background in cognitive psychology had exposed me to the possibility of human intelligence being transferred to computers via future developments in the field of artificial intelligence (AI). No, what surprised me was where the ideas were found, and from whom they were coming.

This was a paper written not by some underemployed computer science graduate student, but, according to his one-paragraph bio, by a professor of English at Penn State University. It appeared not as a posting to some science fiction newsgroup on the Internet, but in the background essays prepared for a program presented at the 1992 American Libraries Association (ALA) summer conference. In this scholarly, respectable context the transfer of human intelligence into the digital realm was being presented not as a conjectural possibility, but as a virtual certainty, just waiting for the necessary technological puzzle pieces to fall into place.

Professor Seesholtz's paper was just one of many prepared for a presentation that featured Hans Moravec (roboticist and author of "Mind Children: The Future of Robot and Human Intelligence"), David Brin (author of "Earth"), and Bruce Sterling (science fiction writer in the "cyberpunk" tradition). The presentation was targeted at librarians and other information science professionals who would be attending the ALA conference. Most of the papers had been written by professionals in those fields.

Reading through these papers, I was struck by the number of times I kept running across the same ideas, written by different people from various backgrounds and locales. Paper after paper echoed the same eerie certainty about the future of the man-machine interface: computers would think; they would think *for* us, they would think *through* us. "What do these people know that I do not?" I wondered. "Who and/or what has been selling them this vision of the future?"

Virtual Reality

When Jaron Lanier coined the term "virtual reality" in the early 1980s, he was trying to describe his vision of the future of the man-machine interface. It would be an immersive three-dimensional world, a shared digital realm, where man could interact with man and machine—creating, exploring, searching the vast storehouses of man's collective knowledge base. By Lanier's estimates, the ultimate realization of this technological vision could take hundreds of years—perhaps a millennium—of technological and cultural innovation and adaptation. The dream is a virtual world where man can interact seamlessly with the information storage capabilities and computational miracle of the digital computer. Ultimately, it is a world where man can express his creative power unhindered by the constraints of our sorry material existence, unhindered even by the constraints of language into which we are now forced to compress and mold our thoughts. The virtual interface of the future will tap directly into the thought patterns of our minds, allowing a form of communication that Lanier called "post-symbolic communication"[2]—that is, communication unfiltered by the grid of a symbolic translation scheme such as language.

Ah, it is a wonderful dream. Meanwhile we have virtual reality of the present and near future. It involves a techno-kludge of three-dimensional displays, gloves, and suits that translate body motions into computer commands, "virtual mice," "virtual keyboards," eye-tracking schemes, voice recognition schemes, and everywhere, *virtual hype*. No matter, virtual reality-mongers from all quarters have already proclaimed the new reality the answer to everything from world peace to kitchen remodeling (it is already being used for kitchen remodeling). But what should not be missed, amid the noise and confusion of the building project just underway, is that the proposed platform for the man-machine interface has switched decisively from the realm of man to the realm of machine; from the *real*, for lack of a better adjective, to the *virtual*.

The Robot Is Waiting

The "robot" of olden days (that is, anything up until about 1984) was a machine that clanked and rattled around the house, factory, or spaceship—doing its best to pretend to be man and perform manlike tasks. Alvin Toffler, in his 1970 classic *Future Shock*, however, predicted the imminent appearance of the humanoid robot:

> At that point [the point of having created robots that are indistinguishable from man] we shall face the novel sensation of trying to determine whether the smiling, assured humanoid behind the airline reservation counter is a pretty girl or a carefully wired robot. The likelihood, of course, is that she will be both.[3]

As it turns out, the human body is more of an engineering feat than once imagined. While robots have grown increasingly sophisticated over the last 25 years, we now see that they have a long, long way to go before anyone mistakes an ATM for a bank teller. What has turned out to be more plastic is man's ability to enter the artificial world of the computer.

If current trends are any indication, the pretty girl and the airline reservation counter she stands behind will both have gone "virtual" long before things ever get to the stage of humanoid robot development that Toffler envisions (if in fact they *ever* do). The "robot" of the virtual future is a computer mind linked to a virtual "body," and we will probably be using a virtual body when we interact with it. Mohammed is going to the mountain; man is going to the machine. Pygmalion, tired of waiting for an answer to his prayers, has decided to become a stone. The robot has arrived, and it is sitting on your desk.[4]

The Birth of Cyberspace

> "Coming into the Virtual World, we inhabit Information. Indeed, we become Information. Thought is embodied, and the Flesh is made Word. It's weird as hell."—John Perry Barlow[5]

The interlinking of computers around the world has been going on in relative obscurity since the late 1960s. It is only recently, with the curious glut of media attention on the "information superhighway" (super-hypeway), that the possibilities inherent in this worldwide communication network have become the object of popular fascination. The Internet, the oldest and most important of the computer networks, began in the mid-1960s as the ARPANET (some old-time Internet residents refuse to yield to modern trends, and still refer to the network by its original name). ARPANET was a federally sponsored project to link computers by telephone to allow military scientists to exchange information. In November 1969, scientists at UCLA tested the first "node"* in the ARPANET by sending a message to San Francisco, and the network was born. By mid-December, the network had four nodes; by mid-1970 the number had grown to ten. Today there are more than three million nodes in the Internet, and the number is growing exponentially. More than a million nodes were added in the first half of 1994 alone.[6]

This Internet and other computer networks like it are the platform on which a true virtual reality will be built. But like a framework without any covering, the "Net," until recently, has been mainly devoid of images, a protean world that could be inhabited but not seen. It was a world waiting for the lights to come on.

This world has been christened "cyberspace," a name given to it by cyberpunk novelist William Gibson in his visionary book *Neuromancer* (1984). Prior to its recent explosion of popularity, cyberspace had been a rather private community, a somewhat anarchic enclave of scientists and other academics exchanging scholarly information and discussing everything under the sun in the newsgroup discussion lists. Also participating were a smattering of disaffected techno-oriented Generation-X'ers, hacking and cracking and adding their own views to the encyclopedic discussion lists.

All this is changing now, however, and rapidly. As PCs (microcomputers) become more powerful, their interface with the Internet (or Net) becomes increasingly more graphical,

---

*A "node" is any network device that has an electronic address on the network.

and the tools available to access the Net become increasingly more sophisticated. Perhaps as a result of the improved interface, and definitely as a result of the increased number of commercial networks now providing Internet access (such as America Online, Prodigy, and CompuServe), the number of new users finding their way into the Net is skyrocketing. The World Wide Web (WWW), an Internet tool that presents information in a graphical, hypertext-based format,* has become the hot ticket.

As more and more "Internauts" sign up for the ride, climb aboard a "web browser," and fire off to the far reaches of the Net, old-time residents worry that the continual influx of users threatens to fundamentally change the nature of cyberspace. Novices take up precious "bandwidth" in the discussion lists with their newbie questions and make egregious breaches in netiquette.** Worse, the economics of the net will have to change. The free ride that many netizens have enjoyed is coming to an end. As the maintenance and support of the network becomes a more substantial issue, government and the telecommunications industry will battle it out to determine who foots the bill and who maintains control. The result of any outcome will almost certainly mean the increased bureaucratization of the Net. But there is no turning back. The doors of cyberspace have been thrown open, and the world is coming to the Net, ready or not.

Beyond 3-D

The World Wide Web adds sounds and pictures to the Internet. But it does not yet qualify as a true virtual reality interface. What is still needed is the ability to provide an "immersive 3-D" visual experience: the user should experience the Net as a location, seen in three dimensions from the vantage point of an "inhabitant" of the virtual world. This type

---

*Hypertext is a means of linking information based on key words or topics.

**Net etiquette.

of interface has been pioneered in the flight simulators and other training devices used by the military and has recently found its way into mass-market gaming machines. The leap into the world of the PC (microcomputer) should not be far behind.

Even this, however, will provide only the minimum requirements for the type of experience being sought by the virtual reality visionaries. Some, for example, imagine future technological advances that will allow a machine to tap directly into the thought processes of a human brain. Imagine a database search engine coupled to a "mind-reading" interface of this sort. The users of such a system merely think about the information they would like to find, and the machine retrieves it from its own database—perhaps even inserting the retrieved information back into the user's mind at the location the user would expect to find it if it had been retrieved from his or her own memory banks. The effective outcome for the user would be as though all the information in the machine's database were actually contained in the user's own mind.

Sound far-fetched? Of course it does. So did color TV at one time. The question is, "Is it possible?" Only time will tell. But at least one leading Silicon Valley firm is doing research into developmental neurophysiology with the aim of producing structures in the brain that will allow this sort of direct linkup between humans and machines.

The ultimate goal, the Holy Grail of the virtual reality intelligentsia, however, appears to be the more or less *complete* transfer of the human intellect into the virtual realm. The end product of such a transfer would be a completely independent intellect, a "persona analog" that starts as a copy of a "biological intelligence" (a "bio-I"), but proceeds to "evolve" along its own independent path as a "cyber-intelligence" (a "cyber-I"). Whether such a being can actually be created is the question of the day. But whether or not there can ever be a complete transfer of the human to the virtual realm, what cannot be questioned is that man is in the midst of a very marked, and remarkable, entry into the realm of the machine.

Virtual Man

The trend toward the increasing "virtuality" of the man-machine interface is an important one. It may, in fact, be tangible evidence of a change in underlying assumptions about what man is, and the nature of reality itself. Or it may be a strong factor in *effecting* that change. But whatever it is—the chicken or the egg—it represents at its core the triumph of the virtual over the created reality. What man is is a question that has only two answers worth considering: he is either a created being, or a product of mindless evolution. The answer we choose reveals much about our view of the whole nature of reality.

The book of Genesis tells us that man was created: "So God created man in his own image, in the image of God he created him; male and female he created them" (Genesis 1:27 RSV). Evolution, on the other hand, tells us that man is the result of an almost impossibly long series of accidents—the collective "wisdom" of eons of mutation and selection.

Genesis tells us that man is a finished work—the consummating work of a good creation (Genesis 1:31). Evolution, in contrast, tells us that man is the expression of a process that has no known beginning, no guiding purpose other than survival, and no known destination. According to this view, any path of divergence is as good as any other, so long as it produces viable offspring.

Evolution, then, places no special importance on the human being. The only truly special thing about the human being—the only *remarkable* thing—is that he has achieved self-consciousness. If this consciousness now exists, there are no rules that preclude it from being involved in the next step of the evolutionary process. The human being, according to this view, is just a "Mr. Potatohead" with parts that we can mix and match as we please. If virtual reality, or any other reality for that matter, will serve us better than the current version, then hooray and off we go. Life will be blissful in the New World, with perhaps only an occasional return to stock up on Jolt! Cola. Imagine a world without hangnails! The stakes are, of course, potentially much higher: *omniscience, omnipresence* (or at least "telepresence"), and *immortality.*

Now hear what God has to say on the matter: "Shall the potter be regarded as the clay; that the thing made should say of its maker, 'He did not make me'; or the thing formed say of him who formed it, 'He has no understanding'?" (Isaiah 29:16).

The humanist-evolutionist paradigm that currently reigns supreme has no ultimate use for questions such as, "Is it wise to attempt to change the form of human being?" It may be a question that is pondered as an interesting problem from the standpoint of psychology, or ethics, or even sociology. The essential question, however, has already been answered. The clay has, in effect, said of the Maker, "He did not make me." The thing formed has said of Him who formed it, "He has no understanding." With the question of accountability to a Maker out of the way, there is no brake to stop the thing made from tinkering with its own form.

Descartes Revisited

All this brings us back to the original question: could a human being actually be "downloaded" into the realm of virtual reality? The possibility may not be as far-fetched as it sounds, if one necessary assumption is allowed. The necessary assumption is this: *the essential "beingness" of a human being is the mind of the individual.* The brain, then, is the organic structure that houses all of that which is truly human. Everything else— feet, legs, arms, torso, and so forth—is simply an evolutionary convenience to allow the human being to exist in one specific set of externally defined constraints (that is, physical reality).

With this assumption in place, the problem of replacing the current mode of human existence with another mode is therefore reduced to just this: *finding an alternative structure to house the mind*. Neural net research, a branch of artificial intelligence (AI), has been working on just that problem, with some success. Neural nets are complex networks of interrelated data that are able to "learn" from presented stimuli. They are modeled after the human brain, and appear to mimic its behavior in acquiring, storing, and interrelating information. Hans Moravec, in his book *Mind Children*,[7] discusses the theory that one day it will be possible to "download" a mind into a sufficiently sophisticated neural net and produce an independent, conscious cyberspace intelligence—a "Cyber-I." The intelligence thus produced will, by virtue of the assumption stated above, be equivalent to the one from which it was downloaded.

A full critique of this position is beyond the scope of this chapter.[8] However, one point must be noted: it completely ignores or denies the element of spirit in the makeup of the human being. It is a fundamentally mechanistic view of the nature of life: life is mind, and merely amounts to organized patterns of neurons colliding. In contrast, Genesis tells us that life comes from God, who is Spirit: "Then the Lord God formed man of dust from the ground, and breathed into his nostrils the breath of life; and man became a living being" (Genesis 2:7).

The Image of the Beast

Life and death are the final enigmas. Throughout the ages, man has wrestled with his inability to create life, and his powerlessness to prevent its ending. Only one man has ever experienced death and overcome it—Jesus Christ the Lord. Even in this century, with all the amazing growth of man's ability to see into the mysteries of time, space, and matter, we are still humiliated before the task of creating a life-form as simple as an ant, or even a bacterium. God seems to have reserved for Himself the power to create life and to overcome death. Maybe it is because of this obvious limit on the extent of human powers that our mythology is replete with the dangers of man creating life. In Jewish folklore, the Golem is the creature of man's creation, loosed on the earth to wreak havoc. In the 20th century, Mary Shelley's Frankenstein is the model: *the creature born of technology who turns on and destroys the creator.*

This sense of foreboding and danger is not absent in the present debate over the possibility of creating "virtual man." Roger Penrose, professor of mathematics at Oxford University and author of the best-selling *The Emperor's New Mind,* is one of those voicing an alarm. Reviewing Moravec's book *Mind Children,* in the *New York Review of Books,* Penrose uses the word "nightmare" to describe Moravec's proposed "downloading" scenario. Moravec responds:

> As the words "frightening" and "nightmare" in your review suggest, intelligent machines are an emotion stirring prospect... Our emotions were forged over eons of evolution, and are triggered by situations, like threats to life or territory, that resemble those that influenced our ancestor's reproductive success. Since there were no intelligent machines in our past, they must resemble something else to incite such a panic. . . .[8]

Maybe. Or maybe they represent something from our future. God, in His Word, has warned man about things to come in a time when the seeds of man's rebellion will have come to full flower. Consider this passage from the book of Revelation:

> Then I saw another beast which rose out of the earth. . . . It works great signs, even making fire come down from heaven to earth in the sight of men; and by the signs which it is allowed to work . . . it deceives those who dwell on earth, bidding them make an image [of] the beast . . . and it was allowed to give breath to the image of the beast so that the

image of the beast should even speak, and to cause those
who would not worship the image of the beast to be slain.
(Revelation 13:11-16)

Those on earth are deceived into making an image of the
beast, an image of a man. The second beast is "allowed" to
give breath to the image. *The image speaks!* Try as I might to
resist the temptation to interpret this notoriously difficult
book in ways that are only applicable to this point in history, I
cannot resist making the following observation: it seems to me
that what John warns of here in terms of a "talking image" is
frighteningly similar to the "Cyber-I" of virtual reality fantasy.
An image of a man, a downloaded replica of a human mind,
given the ability to speak—that is, given the ability to think
and communicate as an independent intelligence. All who
will not worship this image are to be eliminated.

The Word Became Flesh

"In the beginning was the Word, and the Word was with
God, and the Word was God. . . . And the Word became
flesh and dwelt among us . . ." (John 1:1,14a).

The Bible records several amazing aspects of the relationship between God and man, but none more amazing than
this: that the very co-eternal Word became like one of us. Man
has been created in such a way, in the image of God, that God
Himself could inhabit this flesh. The Creator entered into His
own creation, and became one of us. In His wisdom, God was
able to pull off this feat, and the result was the salvation of the
world. Maybe the record of this transaction, the Old and
(especially) the New Testaments, should have been prefaced
with the warning: "The following acts have been performed by
almighty God. Do not attempt to do this at home."

Through virtual reality, man sees perhaps an opportunity
to perform a similar act—to fashion a world of his own design,
and then to inhabit that world as one of its created beings.
The imagined gospel of the new world might say: "And the

Flesh became virtual and dwelt among us." What would the outcome be of such an event? I am afraid that what I see being voiced by the various representatives of the artificial intelligence and library-information science communities is just a techno-variation on the age-old gnostic dream—escape from the bondage of this fleshly existence into . . . what? The world of the electron?

When God came to be with us in the person of Jesus the Christ, He assumed life in the flesh *in its entirety*—conception, birth, childhood, adolescence, maturity, and death. Speaking to the Jews of His day, in language calculated to offend, Jesus said: "I am the living bread which came down from heaven; if any one eats of this bread, he will live for ever; and the bread which I shall give for the life of the world is *my flesh*" (John 6:51, emphasis added).

This is the basis of our hope—that God from the realm of spirit became a man of flesh, one like us, not that man from the realm of flesh will become a virtual god.

4

THE FAUSTIAN BARGAIN—

COMPUTERS AND
HUMAN POTENTIAL

Brooks Alexander

——————— OVERVIEW ———————

What was the Faustian bargain? In the classic legend, Faust sold his soul to the Devil for an irresistible package of self-enhancing powers, including an extra 24 years of life. In the end, he lost his soul in what he realized too late was a futile bargain in what started out as a simple quest for knowledge.

Can we stand back from the flashy technology that has besieged us and question what is really going on? What are the real prospects for human betterment? Will we actually participate in our own conscious evolution? Or will we slip into various cocoons of pleasure, self-absorption, and quests for godlike powers—alternate realities of our own creation—that will lead us collectively down a darker path? Brooks Alexander probes these issues by looking for historical barometers that reflect on these perplexing issues—the primary barometer being the ageless wisdom of Scripture.

The so-called "computer revolution" has been underway for almost half a century now. (The term "cybernetics" was coined in 1947 by Norbert Weiner of the Massachusetts Institute of Technology.) If you take your impressions of reality from the mainstream media, however, you might think it began just a few years ago. Only recently have the subjects of cyberspace, computers, virtual reality, and the information superhighway attracted much media attention—but once the attention began, it turned to a media frenzy. To say the subject has been widely covered in recent years would be a gross understatement. The explosion of information about the information-explosion is one of the ironies of our time.

Not the *only* one, however. Here is another: we know more today than it was even possible to know a mere few years ago. There is a staggering amount of information at our disposal, just waiting for our command to come forth and display itself on our computer screens. Yet, *knowing more* than before, we *understand less* than ever. We are so preoccupied by counting trees that we cannot make sense of our local grove, much less the forest it is part of. Despite the glut of information about computers, it is becoming more difficult than ever to understand their real impact on our lives. One reason for this is that

the incessant innovation in computer technology and software tends to entangle our attention in the present moment.
Like other forms of information overload, relentless novelty
has the effect of numbing our attention and narrowing it
down to the manageable details of the ongoing process of
change.

The "computer revolution," however, cannot be understood outside a context that includes both the past and the
future as well as the present. Unfortunately, that kind of
understanding is beyond our grasp. Our understanding of the
past is sketchy at best; our understanding of the present is virtually nil; our fanciful understanding of the future amounts to
little more than self-serving speculation. As Otto Zeit notes,
"What some have called 'futurism' is not a science at all, but a
forum for technocrats to swap fantasies of social engineering."[1]

As to the past, we do have some knowledge of our history
in relation to computers. We know their military origins, their
early, awkward, civilian applications, their increasing power
and decreasing size, and their expanding presence in every
aspect of our lives. The body of information and comment on
that process is large and growing, even at the popular level.
There are several literary (and video) versions of what we
could call the "Chronicles of Silicon Valley." We know how the
personal computer was invented, who the principal perpetra-
tors were, how they dreamed, how they schemed, how they
jockeyed among themselves, how their business grew, how it
spawned other businesses, and so forth. That sort of information is available in elaborate, often gossipy detail.

Drowning in Data

The irony is that all our historical knowledge does not
help us to understand what is going on today—or to foresee
where we are headed. Despite our fascinating catalog of trees,
the forest (*that is,* the developing influence of computers on
our lives) remains uncharted and is probably unchartable.

Trying to interpret the "computer revolution" resembles a problem in quantum physics. At the subatomic level, one cannot measure a particle's position and velocity simultaneously; that is one of the little things that makes reality unpredictable to our minds. Likewise, at the macro-level of computer influence and social change, one cannot describe the current state of things and keep up with their ongoing development at the same time. Events are happening so fast that it is impossible to stay abreast of them and write about them simultaneously. By the time one has paused long enough to put thoughts into words and words onto paper, the reality one is writing about has surpassed both the facts gathered *and* one's analysis of them. Even such an experienced and knowledgeable thinker as Jacques Ellul has struggled with this problem—and acknowledged defeat in the face of it:

> My first intention was to write a book on all aspects of the impact of the computer on society . . . but I was too late. The world of computers was evolving so fast that I was always two years behind. I could never catch up. I thus abandoned . . . the whole project of clarifying the computer jungle and its relations to our world. I obviously never succeeded in mastering the material. It slipped through my fingers as soon as I thought I had grasped it.[2]

If the present we live in is too complex and slippery to describe, then the future yet to arrive is even more so. We cannot foresee the results of our computers any more than Gutenberg could foresee the results of his printing press—and for the same reasons. One reason is that we are just now at the beginning of the process that we are trying to see to the end of. The changes we are trying to grasp are still unfolding around us; we can only *perceive* them in part because they are only *present* in part.

That much is obvious to common sense. A more basic (and less obvious) reason for our difficulty is that what we are really trying to understand is our own nature. In the end, the computer, like all technology, is about empowering the human will (that is, amplifying human nature)—in all of its manifestations. In trying to understand the computer, then, we are really trying to understand ourselves, and to understand our own impact on the world.

Technology and Social Change

Unfortunately, self-understanding has eluded us ever since we were thrown out of Eden—and there is no evidence that we have gotten better at it over time. In fact, the evidence shows that in case after case we have remained either oblivious or indifferent to the dangers of increasing the potency of the errant human will. The history of technology shows that over thousands of years we have devised increasingly powerful ways of transforming the world into our own image. History also shows that we have been totally unprepared to deal with the consequences we thus set in motion, and have been taken by surprise by them every time.

In 1964 Marshall McLuhan told us that we are changed by the things we make, and we begin to resemble the things we use. "We become what we behold," he said. "We shape our tools, and thereafter our tools shape us." The list of history's culture-changing inventions begins with fire and the wheel, and runs through writing, gunpowder, printing, steam power, internal combustion, electrical power, the telephone, nuclear power, television, and now computers and high-speed information processing. All these technological advances have carried an invisible price tag: besides fulfilling their immediate promises of power and control, they created vast changes in the conditions of human life and the organization of human society. They restructured social arrangements and remolded social attitudes—often through violence and upheaval. And those changes always caught us flat-footed. We have *never* been able either to foresee or to prepare for the long-range results of our own behavior.

The invention of writing illustrates the complex relationship between technology and cultural change. Writing probably originated as a way of keeping records of material resources—that is, as an accounting device. Writing began, in effect, as a business tool. But its effects did not stop with revolutionizing business practice. In the end, writing destroyed the culture of oral tradition and the whole order of society that went with it. Basic social roles were reshuffled. The priests who memorized and recited the "tribal encyclopedia" became irrelevant. Their societies—defined by the oral transmission of knowledge—disappeared or were transformed overnight. Whole classes fell from social grace and new classes rose to replace them. Things formerly valued were now discarded, and things formerly unheard of were now esteemed. The magnitude of those social changes is almost beyond conception—and they were just the beginning.

In preliterate tribal cultures, learning was collective and relational: knowledge was passed on by speaking and hearing, from one person to another. With the advent of writing, however, knowledge could be made into a permanent record. *The transient spoken word could be frozen into a form that was available any time, not just when it was uttered. Now, learning and thinking could be individual and continuous, rather than communal and periodic.* The invention of writing made possible the very concept of individuality as we know it.

Thus, the far-reaching and entirely unforeseen effect of writing was to detribalize Western man. It broke the grip of the tribal group on the power of information. It led directly to the emergence of new and higher political entities—that is, the city-states of Mesopotamia, Egypt, and later, Greece. It also led, of course, to a new concentration of power (politically, economically, and religiously) in the hands of those who were masters of the new medium—namely, those who could read and write.

Writing brought even more changes. It is the basis of literature by definition, and so established the foundation for philosophy. By giving concrete form to revelation, it created scripture, and made possible the broad dissemination of the knowledge of God. It also made science possible. In an oral culture, knowledge is mythic, communal, and initiatory. Once information is freed from the constraints of oral transmission, individuals can seek knowledge systematically. They can record their own experience, survey their record at leisure, and interpret it for themselves—quite apart from rituals of communal indoctrination.

Looking for the Future

All those social changes were double-edged, of course, in the sense that they produced disruption and suffering as well as empowerment and happiness—even by human standards, and more or less in equal measure. By biblical standards, they produced evil as well as good. For example, writing helps to spread both the verities of revelation and the errors of human speculation. As part of that "existential ambivalence," many of the changes that writing unleashed worked their way through society in a process of conflict and turmoil.

All the results described above seem obvious in retrospect. Yet none of them were foreseen at the time (indeed, they were not even seen as such when they were happening). We are too intoxicated with the promises of our technology to see beyond the immediate (or projected) applications of its power. Unfortunately, obsessive attention to trivial detail has become a habit of thought with us. Throughout history we have signally failed to grasp the larger meaning of every technological advance we have invented so far—up to and including the computer. To date, our record of historical self-understanding has been one of unrelenting failure. Humans create their conditions and they create their times. If they do not understand themselves, they will understand nothing, including their times.

Can we hope to do any better today? Can we hope to understand the advent of computers better than our ancestors understood the advent of writing? Can we understand the information superhighway any better than our own parents understood TV? Surprisingly, the answer is—*perhaps*. It all depends on how we proceed.

One thing at least is certain—we will only add to our confusion and misunderstanding if we try to understand the cultural impact of computers by focusing *on computers themselves*. If experience teaches us anything, it teaches us that it is a fool's errand to look for the *results* of technology by studying the *instruments* of technology. We cannot understand the implications of our machines by studying the machines themselves. Technology enables us to *do* certain things. By thinking about the technology itself, we gain an idea of what we are *able* to do, and thus can decide what we *want* to do. But no amount of thinking about technology will tell us the results that will follow once we have actually *done* it. The reality always exceeds our expectations (even our most "expert" expectations), precisely because our fascinated focus on the instruments themselves is nearsighted and misleading. Thinking about our gadgets can only tell us what will happen when we use them; it can never tell us what will happen afterwards.

The limitations of instrumental analysis can be easily illustrated. Consider the impact of gunpowder on warfare and society. Military men of the fourteenth century consciously tried to adapt their strategies to the potential of their new weapon. Some thought ahead, and imagined how the cannon and other firearms could be improved, especially as to their range and rate of fire. They tried, in other words, to sense the present and future potential of their technology and exploit it. In some short-term, limited ways, they were enormously successful. Moated castles and fortified strongholds fell easily before artillery bombardment, and military tactics soon made the most of that increasingly evident fact. Few of the warrior-class, however, saw any implications of their weaponry beyond the conduct of their next battle. No one saw the vast social crisis they were stirring up with their new powers of destruction. The coming of cannons meant an end to feudalism because it meant an end to the defensive fortresses that were the center of feudal life. The castle was the tangible, architectural hub of feudalism's complex social system. Once the castle was rendered indefensible, feudalism was rendered *de facto* defunct.

No one at the time had a clue, however, that those changes were happening. They were too busy figuring out how to apply their new technology in ways that would kill people and break things more efficiently. They could not anticipate the larger results of their firearms because they were thinking about the firearms themselves, and about their immediate application. In a similar way, no one during the "age of steam" understood the social or cultural implications of the "industrial revolution" because they were too wrapped up in thinking about the machines themselves, and about how they could be used.

The same challenge faces us today in our thinking about computers. The irony is that we cannot hope to foresee the results of computers unless we back away from computers themselves. We must look beyond the instruments to the choices we make in creating and using them. And we must look to the universal human factors that shape the making of those choices to begin with. We must go back to *how* we perceive the problems that confront us, and *why* we try to solve them as we do.

We must begin, in other words, with the fundamentals of our own nature. Technology cannot change who we are, but it can and does change the impact of who we are on the world around us. If we can get a handle on our own nature, we have some hope of bringing our behavior under control. If not, we are condemned to lurch from crisis to crisis—propelled by self-will but protected from self-understanding by delusion and denial.

Square One: Ourselves

Delusion arises when we inflate the potential of technology into a fantasy of imagined outcomes, without factoring in the realities that will actually govern the outcome. At the root of delusion, therefore, lies denial. Denial makes delusion inescapable. When we suppress knowledge that would challenge our fantasies or constrain our desires, we insure that our fantasies will remain unfulfilled and our desires will remain unsatisfied. Denial itself comes from the deep self-division we all inherit as part of our human nature. Because we are self-divided (ambi-valent), all our works are ambivalent. This is especially true of technology, which magnifies our ambivalent nature in extraordinary ways.

This is not a novel observation. Many writers have addressed the so-called "ambivalence" of technology. The naive view is that technology itself is inherently neutral, and the goodness or badness of its results depends entirely on how it is used—and especially on the motives with which it is used. Jacques Ellul summarizes this view and thrusts it rather rudely aside:

> From an elementary standpoint the ambivalence of techniques has often been stressed (as in my study in 1950). Techniques can have both good and bad effects. . . . It is often added quietly that everything depends on the use one makes of technique. With a knife one can peel an apple or kill one's neighbor. I tried to show that this comparison is absurd and that technique carries with it its own effects quite apart from how it is used. . . . If we want to know what the issue is when we speak about technique, we must begin by eliminating the futile argument about its use. . . . No matter how it is used, it has of itself a number of positive and negative consequences. This is not just a matter of intention.[3]

Ellul says we must not only notice the ambivalence of technology, we must analyze it. We must see its dynamics as they really are. As a basis for doing so, Ellul advances four propositions, all more or less verified by the common experience of life:

First, all technical progress has its price.

Second, at each stage it raises more and greater problems than it solves.

Third, its harmful effects are inseparable from its beneficial effects.

Fourth, it has a great number of unforeseen effects.[4]

Technology and Humanism

Ellul's observations gain strength from the fact that others have come to similar conclusions without sharing either his starting point or his approach. In *The Arrogance of Humanism,* for example, David Ehrenfeld arrives essentially at Ellul's understanding of technological ambivalence by coming from a completely different direction. Ehrenfeld (a Rutgers biology professor) discusses humanism as a form of religious faith.

At the core of the humanist faith, according to Ehrenfeld, is

> a supreme faith in human reason—its ability to confront and solve the many problems that humans face, its ability to re-arrange both the world of Nature and the affairs of men and women so that human life will prosper . . . humanism elevates our inventiveness to divine levels and celebrates it as infallible.[5]

Ehrenfeld does not start out to discuss technology as a topic, but the issue is soon raised by his critique of our faith in human reason. After all, reason always tries to "confront and solve our problems" through the application of technique and technology. Ehrenfeld's most important insight is his observation that when we try to use technology to solve any large-scale problem (such as the fouling of our environment with the "by-products" of technology), we set off a chain reaction of consequences that is depressingly predictable, plainly observable, and routinely explained away.

Ehrenfeld cites evidence to show that by choosing a techno-answer to, say, environmental problems (his example), we lock ourselves into an escalating cycle of partial solutions that are then followed by new problems—some left over from the original problem, and some generated by the technology that was sent to solve it but didn't. Following Eugene Schwartz, in his book *Overskill*, Ehrenfeld refers to this process as the cycle of "quasi-solutions" followed by "residue problems."

There is no mystery about where this cycle comes from or where it leads. Ehrenfeld describes the process in three simple, easy-to-understand stages.

1) No techno-solution to any environmental problem can ever be complete (or come close to it) because a) the complexity of the environment exceeds our knowledge and understanding to begin with; and b) our technology is a crude instrument that can only intervene awkwardly in a complex ecosystem.

2) The incomplete solution ("quasi-solution") then generates new problems, because the technology assembled to solve the initial problem causes problematic "side effects" (a euphemism for "we did not know *this* would happen") of its own. These "residue problems" are then addressed by new techno-solutions. Each new round of quasi-solutions produces, in turn, a new set of residue problems—which, of course, increases the complexity, the difficulty, and the expense of trying to deal with them. Finally, the problems proliferate faster than solutions can be found to correct them.

3) Our misguided quest for control thereby spirals ironically out of control. But in the process it produces three certain results: a) we *will not* solve the problems we set out to address; b) we *will* create many new problems along the way; and c) most ominous of all, we will also create a cumbersome, expensive, and intrusive bureaucracy to *administer* the stacked layers of corrective technology, added to partial solutions, derived from defective analysis, *and so forth, ad infinitum.* Ehrenfeld describes a pattern of arrogance and naivete that we recognize all too well. The ordained results of that combination (the two always seem to go together) are pride and

bungling, blindness and stumbling, producing disasters in the name of relief.

Ehrenfeld echoes Ellul's discourse on the ambivalence of technology. Both men clearly see and plainly say that all forms of techno-power work to produce both good *and* bad effects. That happens unavoidably because of the inherent flaws and limits of human nature.

Scripture and Understanding

Ellul is a professing Christian. Ehrenfeld is a Jew who plainly takes the biblical worldview seriously. Their converging views should encourage us to consider the *source* of their insight—that is, the Bible. Does the Bible have anything to say about the ambivalence of technology? In fact, it does. It has a great deal to say about the ambivalence of human nature in general (which is fundamental), and its language says something about the nature of technology in particular. (See Appendix A, "Technology and the Fall.")

According to the Bible, there are two relevant facts to understand about human nature: 1) we are created in the image of God; and 2) we are fallen. Because we are made in the image of God, we are creative, dynamic, and purposeful. Because we are fallen, all these qualities are routinely applied in the pursuit of ungodly ends. The net result of those two facts is that all of our thoughts and all our acts express *both* sides of our nature at once.

From a biblical standpoint, therefore, the ambivalence of technology is inevitable. It is the result of empowering the fallen will to act in a fallen world. Because of our self-division, whenever we exercise power in the world, both sides of our nature will be at work to produce their respective results. The greater the power given to the human will, the greater the blessings it will dispense, *and* the greater the damage it will leave in its wake. It is spiritually impossible to have one without the other, because the fall has made us into something we were never created to be—beings divided against ourselves and opposed to our Creator, constantly in conflict with our own created nature, and constantly in friction against God's created world.

With that insight, we come to the threshold of understanding. If we can comprehend ourselves, we may thereby understand our times. If we know *what* the fall is, and *how* it skews our purposes, we may be able to anticipate *how* our technologies amplify our double nature.

The fall has many aspects, but three are particularly important in forecasting the fruits of technology. The three salient aspects are: 1) our obsessive drive for control (and its Siamese twin, the need to dominate); 2) our general inclination toward decay and decline (and our general disinclination to resist the process); and 3) our reflexive impulse of moral evasion and denial (we never want to call it "decay," or to take responsibility for our part in it).

Even at first glance, we can see that this collection of qualities is a surefire recipe for producing a series of corrupt and tyrannical governments, enforced in the name of righteousness (which, by the way, *has* been a prevailing pattern in human affairs). If we unpack the fall even further, however, we can see that it influences every aspect of our lives individually. Each of the three fallen factors—control, corruption, and denial—is personally working in all of us. They affect our personal view of the world, and therefore determine how we react to the world. In other words, the fall warps both our motives and our behavior. What we want is to understand *how* it does so.

The Obsessive Urge to Dominate

Saint Augustine (A.D. 354–430) understood the fall more thoroughly and more biblically than anyone before him or since, with the possible exception of Adam and Eve. In his monumental *City of God,* Augustine unraveled some of the tangled dynamics of the fall.

According to Augustine, the fall locks us into a deepening cycle of defensive alienation. To get the process rolling, as the third chapter of Genesis indicates, we separate ourselves from God. As the bumper sticker puts it, "If you feel far from God—guess who moved?" By seeking *our* way rather than the ways of God, we find that we have departed from the presence of God. By relying on *our* strength rather than the strength of God, we find that the strength of God has departed from our lives. Suddenly we face an overwhelming world with *only our* strength to rely on. Without God, our strength is transparently inadequate. We are acutely aware of our helplessness and are overcome by existential panic.

Because we sense that our power is inadequate, we compulsively try to assert it, almost as a reflexive act of denial. We do not premeditate that response and cannot control it. It cannot be erased by "enlightenment," educated away, or trained not to happen. The fall has made it a part of our nature.

Our drive to dominate others is the unmistakable stain of that disorder. The one sure way we can create at least the appearance of control is in connection with those of our own kind. We cannot control nature, but we can control (or *pretend* to control) other people. So we try to assert our power first and foremost by subjecting others to our will—even as they do the same to us. Thus, all our relationships are characterized by a sense of insatiable desperation. The basic fact of our inner life is that we are infected with deficiency and fear, to which we involuntarily respond with over-assertion and obsessive self-concern.

The urge to dominate, the rule of violence, and the unjust layering of society are all just parts of that same fallen pattern. Everyone bemoans some part of the pattern, but the pattern as a whole is our own creation. It continues to exist because we continue to sustain it by behaving out of our inherited, primal anxieties—especially in relation to one another. The continual interplay of fallen motives is enough to create the entire structure of human affairs that we know as the fallen "world system." That is as close to the mechanics of original sin as Augustine can bring us, and it is close enough to expose the inner workings of the global system of sin that Augustine called the "Earthly City" (as distinguished from the "City of God").

Computers and the Domination Impulse

What does all this have to do with the impact of computers? Quite a bit. Some implications of Augustine's insight are visible right away. First, it means that the potential of computers for controlling, manipulating, and monitoring people will be explored enthusiastically, and the exploration will be well-funded. All the "Big Brother" features of a computerized society will be eagerly investigated, and many of them will be eagerly implemented—at every level. From the heavens, invisible spy satellites already peer into the open trunk of a car, or through an unshuttered window; they can see in the dark and probe beneath the ground with radar and infrared. Somewhat more down to earth, the city-state of Singapore provides a chilling example of the way sophisticated technocrats can use computers to create a totally managed and monitored society. Government, however, is not the only place the "Big Brother temptation" is at work; the gadgetry of snooping is already well-developed for use in businesses that rely on computers extensively. As Clifford Stoll observes,

> Computers lend themselves to being used as management tools. They can keep track of idle time, number of words typed, number of errors made. Telephone operators must handle a certain number of calls per minute. Secretarial staff face a quota of typing a certain number of insurance claims every hour. A digital dungeon.[6]

Augustine's insight also means that the power of computers in our society will be unequally and unfairly distributed. The more complex computer technology becomes, the wider the gap will become between those who can afford real computing power (mainly governments and large corporations) and those who can only afford to play with the trickle-down of lesser toys. Society always divides into *haves* and *have-nots*—based on the obsession to exercise control and the struggle to dominate. The raw fact is that in any struggle for control, some will prevail and some will not.

In an information society, the basic division will occur between the info-rich and the info-poor, between those with wide access to information and those with limited access, between the cyber-illuminati and the cyber-ignorati. The power shift that is currently underway will give the techno-elite the power to remold society in *their* image, and to shape our social arrangements to fit *their* vision of the ideal polity. It goes without saying that the ideal polity, in the view of the techno-elite, is one that is organized to service the needs of *their* technology and to promote *their own* happiness and general welfare. It should surprise no one but the incurably naive that such an agenda has the "side effect" of creating a new underclass of info-serfs that will toil in the so-called "service industries" to support the technical needs of the information hierarchy and to cater to its personal desires.

Myth Meets Reality

Cyber-enthusiasts protest that this is a jaundiced view. In fact, many of them are confidently expecting the exact opposite to happen. The real impact of the computer revolution, they tell us, will be to "democratize" access to information, and actually *undermine* the power of any presumed "information elite." This optimistic view is based on the potential of computers to provide nearly universal access to their resources, and the *assumption* that this potential will be fulfilled. Techno-optimists envision the new information society as a kind of happy anarchy—a state of benign, unstructured social chaos—in which every individual is empowered to control the circumstances of his life through the medium of his multi-functional computer terminal (or "communications center" in cyber-speak).

Unfortunately, this view ignores all the thorny questions about how the technology will *actually* be used. How much of the potential will be realized, and how much will remain a wistful dream—or even become a destructive delusion? Techno-optimism barely recognizes the question. In addition, techno-optimism seems blind to the very real biases and exclusions that are built into the technology itself. *At its best,* the information superhighway will be as universally accessible as the interstate highway system—that is, anyone with a car can use it. The unstated side of that equation is that those without cars cannot and will not use it. Any technology requires the ability to use its instruments; the opportunity to use them is a *prerequisite* to enjoying the benefits of that technology. "Universal access" is a myth.

The problem is inherent. Every technological advance reshuffles social priorities and rearranges the social hierarchy, rewarding some people and disenfranchising others. Computers simply speed up that process, and they do so because of the nature of their technology, completely apart from the conscious intentions of anyone who uses them. Clifford Stoll describes the exclusionary nature of technocratic culture:

> For all the talk of friendly, open systems, there's no warm welcome for novices. It's up to the user to figure out which system is best, up to the user to install and maintain the software.

> In the same way, the networked community is an exclusive club for the initiated. Too often, there's an established hazing ritual to get online.

> Result: the computing elite claim that theirs is an open, accessible world, while barring outsiders through a liturgy of technology. It's the culture of exclusion . . . engineers

routinely use cryptic labels that mystify the technology and deny access to ordinary people.[7]

Techno-optimists claim that with dedication and good intentions, all these problems can be overcome. The biblical realist responds that *yes*, many things *might* happen, in an imaginary world of consistently sane and compassionate choices. In the real world, however, our choices are made in a state of existential panic, and they most often are made in pursuit of our blind urge to control and dominate. The exclusionary nature of the technology is thus reinforced by our own fundamental motivations—and vice versa—because the technology is a product of our fundamental motivations to begin with.

Will the information society become a stratified world of social perks and power, with whole classes of people relegated to techno-serfdom? Today, that is a redundant question. Never seriously in doubt, the results of our technology are already evident. No forecasting is required, only observation. The unskilled, the undereducated, the poor, the homeless, African-Americans, Hispanics, and women are already being left in the dust of the accelerating revolution. Some writers have noted and lamented that problem, but no one has proposed a viable solution to it. Everything we know suggests that such social gaps tend to widen rather than to shrink.

A Disturbing Look at Our Real Future

David Noble is a vocal critic of "computerism" and the information society. His comments are notable because he bears an impressive set of credentials. He taught at Massachusetts Institute of Technology for nearly a decade and was the curator of industrial automation at the Smithsonian Institution in Washington, D.C. He is considered something of a techno-apostate in the academic community, and it is not difficult to see why. In the passage below, he enumerates the observable socioeconomic results of computerization so far, and the list alone is unnerving. Noble looks at the world with unblinking realism and expresses his vision with devastating clarity.

To see where we are headed requires no voodoo forecasting or futuristic speculation, much less federally funded research. We just need to take a look at where we've been and where we are. The returns are already in on the information age, and the information highway promises merely more of the same, at an accelerated pace.

In the wake of the information revolution (now four decades old), people are working harder and longer (with compulsory overtime), under worsening working conditions with greater anxiety, stress and accidents, with less skills, less security, less autonomy, less power (individually and collectively), less benefits and less pay. Without question the technology has been developed and used to de-skill and discipline the workforce in a global speed-up of unprecedented proportions. And those still working are the lucky ones. For the technology has been designed above all to displace.

Today we are in the midst of what is called a "jobless recovery," symptomatic and symbolic of the new age. Outputs and profits rise without the jobs that used to go with them. Moreover, one fifth of those employed are only part time or temporary employees, with little or no benefits beyond bare-subsistence wages, and no security whatever.

None of this has happened by accident. The technology was developed, typically at public expense, with precisely these ends in mind by government (notably military), finance, and business elites—to shorten the chain of command and extend communications and control (the military origins of the Internet), to allow for instantaneous monitoring of money markets and funds transfer, and to enable manufacturers to extend the range of their operations in pursuit of cheaper and more compliant labor.

For decades we have silently subsidized the development of the very technologies that have been used to destroy our lives and livelihoods, and we are about to do it again, without debate,

without any safeguards, without any guarantees. The calamity
we now confront, as a consequence, rivals the upheavals of the
first industrial revolution two centuries ago, with its untold
human suffering. We are in for a struggle unlike anything any of
us have ever seen before. . . .[8]

In Noble's view, it is needless to wonder and redundant to
ask *how* computers will affect our society. The answers are
already before us, and the news is not good. The only question left is whether we can deal with that news or whether we
will try to rationalize it—continuing to scratch our heads in
bemusement and confusion, and continuing to search for
new answers to displace the answers we do not want to hear.

The Effects of Decay and Decline

The second salient aspect of the fall that determines the
real impact of computers is our general tendency toward
moral and spiritual corruption, and our general disinclination to resist it. In a fallen world, corruption is a natural,
almost mechanical process. We are all familiar with it through
the phenomena of nature. The cycle of death and decay as we
know it is a product of the fall, which distorts a natural, God-
given process of self-renewing change and transformation
into a process of self-destroying breakdown and dissolution.

What is true on the physical level also has its analog in the
higher realms of personality, relationships, collective morality,
and society in general. All these are subject to degradation
over time, through the repeated making of choices that cater
to our own lower tendencies—especially that of seeking our
satisfaction regardless of the consequences. That primal
fallen motivation, multiplied millions of times a day, acts as a
slow corrosive on the bonds of culture and the sinews of
society. Here again, we have a self-reinforcing process, as radical selfishness promotes social breakdown, which encourages
more—*and more extreme*—forms of radical selfishness.

The process, though vast, is not totally impersonal. The
fallen world has its own fallen "ecology," and there are always

those who promote the process of cultural decay because they expect to gain from it. The very nature of decay is to break down existing structures, releasing energy in the process, which the agents of decay then feed on. Biologically, energy is locked up in units of living cells. A piece of meat left in the open air will soon begin to rot, as decay bacteria break down the structure of its tissues. The bacteria flourish, feeding on the energies of life released by the dissolving cells.

Culturally, energies are stored in various institutions such as marriage, the family, the neighborhood, the tribe, the race, the nation, a shared morality, and the like. When the structures of society break down, that locked-up energy is released at large. Much of it manifests immediately in the form of commercial profits generated by merchandising our decline (MTV is a good example). Some of the energy turns into the passion and zeal (and the money) to pump up our culturally radical movements and ideologies. And some of it goes to advance the agendas of those who are cynical enough and skilled enough to work the process of social decay to their personal advantage (this is the "earthly, demonic wisdom" referred to in James 3:15).

What does this have to do with the information superhighway? It has to do with the kind of information that travels on it. We can confidently predict that pornography on the Internet will increase in volume and depravity, as will destructive, violent, hateful, dangerous, and dehumanizing information of every other kind.

The development of television provides an exact analogy of what we can expect from the development of an electronically networked society. In 1939 David Sarnoff of RCA expansively declared, "It is probable that television drama of high caliber and produced by first-rate artists will materially raise the level of dramatic taste of the nation." Fifty-six years later we can see for ourselves the river of repugnant sludge that television entertainment has become—insulting to aesthetics and toxic to the soul.

We are entitled to laugh, therefore, when the cyber-enthusiasts boast that the information superhighway will open up a
spontaneous cultural renaissance and lead to a literary revival.
It will not happen. It is already not happening. Clifford Stoll
comments that the great preponderance of messages on the
Internet are badly written and sloppily organized renditions
of half-baked ideas. He says that much of the "information"
available on-line is a waste of time to read, not to mention the
time wasted in "accessing" it. (Sounds like TV—"500 channels, and nothing on.") Stoll says he will tune into the on-line
discussion groups "the next time I have to spend a week in
traction . . . one of the joys of computers is how they are great
at wasting time that might otherwise be difficult to waste."[9]

Stoll's skepticism is that of an initiate, not an outsider. His
expertise in navigating the networks is unquestioned. (His
first book, *The Cuckoo's Egg*, is the story of how he tracked
down and eventually trapped a German spy ring operating
through the Internet.) Like David Noble, Clifford Stoll simply
tells us what he knows to be the case from watching it
happen—or in this case, *not* happen.

> One of the more pernicious myths of the online world is
> that of a literary revival. . . . Since the networks rely on the
> written word, you'd expect a rebirth of reading and writing.
> The Internet should be a garden for literate, well-trained
> users to take advantage of a new mode of communications.
> . . . The result should be the honing of literary skills and a
> new wave of creative literature.
>
> But instead of an Internet-inspired renaissance, mediocre
> writing and poorly thought-out arguments pour into my
> modem. E-mail and postings to network newsgroups are fre-
> quently ungrammatical, misspelled, and poorly organized.
> After trolling up and down the Usenet . . . I rarely find prose
> that's articulate and creative.[10]

This flood of the banal, the bombastic, and the irrelevant
clutters the information superhighway like junk mail clutters

the postal system. But you can't simply sort it and discard it the way you do with the junk mail that clogs your mailbox. You have to scroll through all of it to get to the good stuff—if *there is* any good stuff, and *if* you can find it. It is irritating and inconvenient, but at least it does not precipitate an immediate social crisis.

The human potential for perversity and degradation, on the other hand, will certainly trap us in an impossible dilemma very soon. This is our inescapable quandary: given the power and scope of the information superhighway, there is no way to avoid toxic levels of information-sewage in society without resorting to totalitarian methods of information monitoring and control.

Neither of those alternatives are acceptable, but before long we will have to actually make the choices that are just facing us today. Issues of free speech versus censorship are already being raised with an urgency that is bound to increase. Of course, this is nothing new. The conflict of free self-expression with the forces of social constraint is as ancient as society itself. The advent of computers, however, intensifies the conflict and magnifies its outcome in ways we are poorly equipped to understand or respond to.

Divided human nature drives the dialectic between personal license and external restraint. Excessive freedom always leads to corrupt and corrupting behavior, because of our fallen center of gravity. Eventually the socially destructive results of such behavior become clear. Society reacts defensively to expunge the decay by fiat and force. We become a society of repression and intrusion to avoid becoming a society of corruption and debility.

The cycle is basically simple. As the process of social decay advances, social institutions lose their power to restrain behavior and to bind people together. Society increasingly atomizes into self-seeking ego units. Depravity and criminality explode, anarchy prevails, disorder descends, and tyranny rises to replace it.

What part will computers play in the currently unfolding version of that cycle? We have already seen how readily computers can be used as instruments of personal surveillance and social control. *Thus computer technology not only brings our social crisis to a head, it also becomes our means of coping with the crisis—a neat package of self-contained historical cause and effect.* That is the closed, reinforcing cycle of fallen human nature expressing itself through the medium of a fallen world. Our fallenness reverberates in a feedback loop. The outcome of that process is gruesomely depicted in St. John's *Revelation*. Apart from the Second Coming, this scenario has no happy ending.

Instincts of Evasion, Philosophies of Denial

"Denial" is the third fallen factor that distorts our technology. G. K. Chesterton said that the fallenness of man is the only Christian doctrine that is empirically verifiable. One persistent and verifiable *result* of our fall is a deep inner compulsion to deny our own fallen nature. Common experience confirms this to us on a daily basis. It usually takes the form of avoiding personal responsibility for our behavior. Psychologists call it "projection." Most people just call it "passing the buck." The Bible describes the first case of it in Genesis 3:11-13. Whatever you call it, the gist of it is to say "the problem is not in here, it's out there."

Plainly, though, if the problem *really is* "in here" (as Scripture insists), then to deny that fact creates a major reality gap. If we cannot begin at the personal level by dealing honestly with our condition, then all our clever efforts at understanding the larger world will only come to naught—or worse, will build delusions that turn against us and create confusion and suffering.

Our fallenness is part of the real world in which we live. If we try to understand the world while avoiding the fall, we will only build an architecture of evasion and denial. Our basic moral avoidance regarding ourselves unavoidably distorts our understanding of everything else—including the rest of creation.

The logic of that process is simple and straightforward: if we insist on asking "why?" but refuse to acknowledge the real "because," we are bound to end up with a bogus "because." Once we embrace the bogus answer, bogus action follows. We develop misguided strategies for dealing with misunderstood problems, while our real problems go unattended. If we cannot admit the truth about ourselves, we can never find the truth about anything else. In the words of de Rougemont,

> One of the reasons confusion is spreading in the world is that we are afraid to face its real causes. We believe in a thousand evils, fear a thousand dangers, but have ceased to believe in Evil and to fear the true Danger. . . . We are never in greater danger than when we deceive ourselves as to the real nature of a threat, and when we summon our energies for a defense against the void, while the enemy approaches from behind.[11]

In the long run, all such systems of denial fail, as do the misguided strategies and deluded expectations based upon them. Some false systems simply lose their credibility over time; others collapse and fall in spectacular fashion. Freudianism and communism come to mind as recent examples—both of them, by the way, crafted explicitly to contradict the biblical view of man. Those particular false ideologies have failed in a publicly visible way. Privately, however, all of us are philosophers of denial. Eventually, our personal systems of moral evasion will collapse as well. Human fallenness is the uncharted reef that will ultimately shipwreck the humanist fantasy—and the reef is not on the chart precisely because of our primary moral denial.

Denial and Idealism

What does our pattern of moral evasion have to do with computers? Some implications are obvious; others are more subtle. In the realm of the obvious, our evasion means we will always embrace our technology by reaching for its "positive potential," blissfully blind to its inevitable fallen consequences. It means, in other words, that mere idealism will always lead us astray, because we cannot factor our own defects into our dreams and ambitions. Specifically, it means that the worst consequences of "computerization" are going to sneak up on us because we are in denial about their source—that is, *ourselves.*

It is folly to believe we can understand ahead of time the problems computers will present; it is a greater and compounding folly to believe we can forestall those problems by means of preventive public policy. By trying to regulate the *symptoms* of human fallenness, we insure that the underlying *cause* of the problem remains untouched. So long as the cause remains untouched, it can generate an infinite variety of symptoms. Even if we succeed in suppressing one set of symptoms, another set will arise to replace it. Trying to cope with the symptoms of the fall from our condition of fallenness is like a classic "Three Stooges" comedy: no sooner do we finally get the top drawer of the dresser shut (after much struggle) than the bottom drawer pops out and bangs our shins. We kneel down to struggle with the bottom drawer, and finally wrestle it shut, only to be banged in the face by the middle drawer—*and so forth,* apparently *ad infinitum.*

The spread of computer technology brings us to another crest in a repeating cycle—a cycle of techno-solutions that turn themselves into problems. Computers are currently undergoing that same cycle—but enormously speeded up. The results of that cycle still remain a matter of uncertainty, but they will not stay that way for long. We will soon find out firsthand how computers can be used to manage and monitor our lives. We can confidently predict this general outcome because our historical pattern of false optimism is both obvious and unbroken—and the pattern will continue unbroken for as long as we continue in our primary denial.

Denial and Gnosticism

In the realm of the not-so-obvious, the impulse of denial has religious implications, as well. The spirit of denial lies at the bottom of Gnosticism, that perennial spiritual counterfeit.

Gnosticism says, in effect, that the problems of this world are built into the material nature of the world. Our wrongness, in other words, comes from the wrongness of what we are made of. We are really pure spirits who are tragically trapped in physical bodies. The gnostic goal is to free the spirit from the fleshly bonds that tangle it in ignorance and delusion.

In the end, the gnostic temptation is another example of the quest to escape the realities of our own condition. It is a classic case of moral and spiritual buck-shuffling: "The problem is not in here, it's out there, in those pesky atoms and molecules."

Today the gnostic dream takes shape as the quest to become a disembodied mind—existing as pure digital intelligence—infinitely free in cyberspace to know, do, or *be* anything the mind can imagine. If you think that sounds like the same vaulting ambition that brought us the Tower of Babel, you are right: "This is what they began to do, and now nothing which they purpose to do will be impossible for them" (Genesis 11:6 NASB). In cyberspace an entity can be anything it wants—male or female, stern or seductive, brilliant or stupid. It can be a complete fantasy—a persona that has no real world counterpart. Does such a "cyber-person" really exist? Can the human self duplicate its identity in the form of an infinitely complex digital code, then manipulate the code—and thus the identity—at will?

Vaporizing the Body

Do these ideas seem outrageous and far-fetched to you? Then you have not tuned into the cyber-culture recently. If you listen to what some of our cyber-poets, cyberpunks, and cyber-pundits are saying, you will begin to sense how thoroughly the fallen impulse of denial drives the gnostic quest to escape the constraints of bodily existence into a virtual world where reality is malleable and freedom is unlimited.

> Virtual Reality is the dream of pure telematic experience. . . . In virtual reality, flesh vaporizes into virtuality as twentieth-century bodies are repackaged with twenty-first-century cybernetic systems for speeding across the electronic frontier.

> The wired body is perfect. Travelling like an electronic nomad through the circulatory flows of the mediascape, it possesses only the virtual form of a multi-layer scanner image. Abandoning the heavy referential history of a central nervous system, the wired body actually grows a telematic nervous system that is freely distributed across the electronic mirror of the Internet. A product of neural tapping and image processing, the wired body is the (technoid) life-form that finally cracks its way out of the dead shell of human culture.

> Technotopia is about disappearances: the vanishing of the body into a relational data base, the nervous system into "distributive processing," and the skin into wetware. As technology comes alive as a distinctive species, we finally encounter the end of (human) history and the beginning of virtual history.[12]

Computers amplify the gnostic option. The association of computers with a gnostic worldview is perfectly natural, even inevitable. Cyberspace provides what seems to be an actual, technically feasible medium in which to realize our ancient gnostic dream—that is, to escape from dependence on the physical world and ascend to the limitless freedom of pure, disembodied intelligence. Through computers, the prospect of practical omniscience beckons, as does the promise of virtual omnipresence, as the mind extends its presence at will across the reaches of the global network.

The cyber-world fits the gnostic mind-set like a glove. Some of the connections between the two virtually call attention to themselves. Original Gnosticism was an elitist religion, based on spiritual technology, and above all on spiritual *knowl-edge*—the "gnosis" from which the gnostics got their name. Computers store and manipulate "knowledge" *par excellence.* Therefore, as the gnostic impulse seeks technological expression, the technology naturally tends to generate tech-gnosis ("cybernetically mediated enlightenment").

The techno-gnostic connection is not just an abstract historical possibility. It exists already and *has existed* from the earliest days of the cyber-culture. The hippie counterculture, especially in its New Age version, has always influenced the thinking of the cyber-pioneers. By now, gnostic spirituality has been thoroughly woven into the way most of the people in Silicon Valley think about computers—and about the world and their place in it. Partly because of its historical association with computers and the computing-elite, neo-Gnosticism has already established itself as an influence in our process of cultural change.

> New Age elements are rife throughout the post-1960's Bay Area culture that laid the groundwork for much of what we call cyberculture. A psychedelic, do-it-yourself spirituality directly feeds the more utopian elements of this Northern California subculture of Virtual Reality designers, computer artists, and computer programmers. . . . For many of these folks, computers are the latest and among the greatest tools available for the achievement of the Aquarian goal: the expansion of consciousness by whatever means necessary.

> But the influence of the New Age movement on cyberculture extends beyond that of the psychedelic fringe. . . . For the more futuristic New Agers, the self is an information-processing entity that changes nature, depending on the information-flows it receives and the various media to which it connects. This emphasis on information-flows stems in part from the New Age role as the religion of the Information Age. It also explains the crucial role played by one particular occult technique: channeling.[13]

Balancing the Discussion

If anyone protests that this has been a one-sided look at the computer revolution, I say, "exactly so." The side I have emphasized is the side being ignored. The optimists, idealists, and gnostic dreamers already have their voice. Our ears are filled to overflowing with their promises. If we need anything, we need a corrective vision. We need someone to say, "Wait a minute—it isn't going to happen this way. We are overlooking something real, and despised reality will take its revenge. Just because we want to fly doesn't mean that gravity has been abolished. Just because we want to escape the pains and constraints of our fallen human condition doesn't mean we can."

Yes, the computer revolution has its positive aspects. Yes, I personally use a computer for word processing (it makes the text wonderfully malleable). For the moment, at least, our technology has given us remarkable ways of turning up the volume on our message and general commentary.

We should not ignore, however, the fact that our double nature means that all our behavior has effects in *both* directions. Because we are made in the image of God, even our evil intentions routinely produce good results as a "side effect." But the fallen will operating in a fallen world has a double advantage in that balance. We are faced with a kind of "Gresham's Law" of the spirit—the effect of our bad intentions seems to drive out the effect of our good ones. The fallen factors tend to reinforce one another, while the godly influences have to establish themselves against the tide.

In the long run, therefore, our fallen center of gravity tends to set the compass for the course of history. In this fallen age, the "image of God" side of our double nature acts mostly as a brake on our worst tendencies and a barrier to realizing our worst possibilities, rather than as an active reforming and cleansing force (cleansing and reformation mostly result from God's direct intervention). That conclusion commends itself to our intelligence not only because it is found in Scripture, but because its proof is found in our everyday lives.

Unfortunately, this clear-eyed vision of reality leads directly to an existential dilemma: if we ignore the fallen factor, we are doubly at its mercy; but if we attend to it, we are quickly brought to despair. What is the answer?

Slouching Toward Dystopia

The bad news is that within the self-contained world of fallen human motives and means, there *is no* real answer. As history progresses, the fallen side of human nature gradually solidifies its hold on human affairs, abetted by technology—a metaphysical metastasis that is occasionally interrupted by episodes of divine judgment, but is never in remission. Nor can we defer the impact of a given technology by refusing to use it ("just say no to computers"). In the larger pattern, the "Amish option" is simply a part of the dialectic by which technology extends its influence.

We try to pretend there are answers, that things are getting better, and that we can yet solve our problems with the wise use of technical means. We disguise our unbroken record of failure in that regard with ideologies of "progress" and "evolution." But they are transparent disguises. Otto Zeit defines progress as "the monotonous repetition of the same human errors at ever higher levels of technical skill."

Our double nature locks us into a downward spiral. There is nothing we can "do" to stop the process, because our "doing" is what the process consists of in the first place. As Jacques Ellul put it,

> In the face of technique, and of our inability to confront it,
> I would say then, with Livy, that we can endure neither our
> evils nor their cures, and with Tacitus, that the weakness of
> human nature means that cures always lag behind evils.[14]

The Bible concludes with the Apocalypse because *that* is the end that fallen human nature inexorably descends to. Human fallenness means denial; denial produces delusion; and delusion leads to disaster. *Welcome to reality.*

The Real Balance

Yet there is an answer after all. From *beyond* the fallen cycle of human cause and effect, providence does intrude. The book of Revelation shows how the force of denial collapses in upon itself to produce an escalating series of judgments. It also shows us that behind those judgments lies God's redemptive purpose.

If any of us have the power to affect events, it will not be by what we *do,* but by who and what we *become.* In our own strength, we can never control our compulsion to assert control. We can never address our fallen condition from within our fallen condition. It takes something *from outside* the world to redeem the world. *We* cannot make that happen, but we *can* link ourselves to the One who already made it happen, the One who already broke into our closed system. The first stage in creating that link is to position ourselves appropriately in relation to our Creator. We are created; He is not. That "gnosis" is the beginning of wisdom—and the beginning of the end for denial and delusion.

PART TWO

Virtual Reality and the
Quest for Digital Godhood

5

VIRTUAL GODS, DESIGNER UNIVERSES

Tal Brooke

OVERVIEW

Only in its infancy, crude forms of virtual reality have just begun to appear in video arcades, movies, and virtual entertainment theaters. The technological wonder of virtual reality—"the Holy Grail of cyberspace"—has appeared just in the nick of time to enter the next millennium. This computer-generated marvel promises to fully duplicate the real world to such an extent that the human mind and senses will not know the difference. Its effects will surpass movies of today to the same degree that digital cinerama surpassed the turn-of-the-century silent screen with its halting motion and grainy film. If virtual reality can provide a breathtaking array of lifelike experiences—with no limits on how surreal or exotic—this same electronic genie might also penetrate the mind in unforeseen ways. It could even introduce a level of human surveillance—indeed governance—that will end cherished freedoms with the suddenness of an earthquake. Beyond entertainment and human enhancement, we need to contemplate what might happen once the switch is engaged and the vast turbines of this technology are turned on.

irtual reality is not just the upper story of cyberspace, it is considered its Holy Grail, for it promises to be a new gateway to unlimited experience—*without apparent consequences.* This makes it a kind of cosmic Rubic's cube of entertainment and pleasure that men have sought throughout the ages. What the mind imagines can be thrust up instantly into existence. And this is surely a godlike power. For magic will have arrived—coming at just the right time to a generation that venerates experience over almost everything else.

When the technology fully comes of age, you will be able to bring any fantasy to life and actually don some superhero's body and dive off the World Trade Center, swooping by windows and waving at astounded onlookers. Or you might bungee-jump from an airplane over the jungles of Sumatra, whooshing toward a smoking volcano till you hover inches above the boiling lava, feeling the adrenaline rush of a lifetime. It will not kill you and you do not have to spend exorbitant amounts of money for the real experience. A child might decide to appear on someone's coffee table the size of an ant, or even wander across the Martian desert in some alien tribal gear.

More sedate folks can have tea at Buckingham Palace with the Queen, feasting with gold cutlery and precious china. Or they might take the Grand Orient Express to Budapest as old Europe passes by. Those who long for youth can be young again . . . for a while. Women in their 20s and 30s can live out some long-cherished dream, such as standing in the place of Greta Garbo while clutching onto Clark Gable and watching the spray of the Victoria Falls—and holding on to this pregnant moment in time that never happened in the real world. Virtual reality intersects human vulnerability, perhaps on some level where desires and longings meet the imagination. And that makes it a formidable mind-machine.

Virtual reality is a kind of scientific magic. It promises to create seamless synthetic illusions that can bend and shape perceived reality like the powerful spells of the great sorcerers of medieval legend. Broomsticks can splinter, clone themselves, and carry pails of water down the spiraling stairs forever in this version of the *Sorcerer's Apprentice.*

The genie that provides the engine for this magical illusion is the computer. As computers grow in power, the spell becomes more convincing and overpowering. Some feel the illusion will eventually surpass reality once there is sufficient power.

The computer has outgrown itself time and again since the halfway point of this century when it was first called *ENIAC* and spread across several giant warehouses of vacuum tubes and electronic components. Yet this giant 1940s monster is barely a glowing ember when compared to today's simplest handheld calculators.

"Deep Blue," the latest computer prototype—a hungry intelligence that can speed through 200 million decisions per second while "seeing" billions of moves ahead—almost beat the world's top chess player, Gary Kasparov, tying him three times and beating him once in a match. Previous computer chess matches were almost no contest for human grand masters. The next prototype to come will be significantly more powerful while the present human victor will feel his waning powers. At some point soon, the creation will be greater than its creator in yet another domain where human intelligence previously reigned uncontested.

Computer visionaries conceived of the computer with far more ambitious purposes in mind than simply playing chess, or keeping track of things like cyberspace, geosynchronous satellites, or the New York Stock Exchange. One long-range purpose has been the mind-machine interface that would provide a means of creating a sense-experience realm so palpable, so immediate and convincing, that it could be called "virtual reality." Part of the vision was the sheer entertainment it would provide. Another was the quest for mind expansion. Other darker visionaries might have seen in it a certain potential for social engineering and mind control—the totalitarian downside.

Aldous Huxley foresaw virtual reality. He also predicted a correspondence between virtual entertainment and mind control in his futuristic novel, *Brave New World*. This novel described "talkie-feelies"—interactive movies that totally immersed audiences in lifelike experiences so intense that they lost themselves in the experience. In Huxley's futuristic world, the masses were gradually being domesticated through entertainment, a kind of mind control that made them livestock in the hands of the "world controllers," a techno-dictatorship. These passive human cattle looked to pleasure as their supreme goal in life, their *raison d'etre*, and they auctioned away their freedoms to the social engineers in exchange for welfare and pleasure. Too intellectually dim to ever see any cause and effect, they had been herded in a slow campaign of gradualism from democracy to technocracy.

Luxor, Las Vegas

An audience is screaming and it sounds like a roller coaster ride as a scene out of *Indiana Jones* fills the television screen on another prime-time documentary about an explosive new technology. A mining train barrels through an underground mine shaft at incredible speed. It is a pure cinerama

roller coaster ride. Surround-sound effects jump out at you—
from metallic braking sounds to crashes and rumbles deep in
the mine. The camera then backs up. What you thought were
riders on the train behind you are a balcony audience in a virtual reality theater. They have been watching the same scene in
3-D cinerama while pitching and rocking on a moving floor.
Clearly the experience is riveting, and it is happening at the
brand-new Luxor Casino, a huge 2,500-room supercasino in
Las Vegas. This towering pyramid has the ultimate entertainment theater at the very top, with virtual reality effects that are
pure state-of-the-art. The audience is giddy by the end of it.

Howard Rheingold, a virtual reality visionary who wrote
Virtual Communities, reports that the three-theater "Secrets of
the Luxor Pyramid" is the biggest thing Douglas Trumbull has
done since he revolutionized the special effects business in
1968 with *2001: A Space Odyssey.* As the wizard credited for special effects in *Close Encounters of the Third Kind* and other block-
busters, Trumbull is one of the few artists capable of creating
virtual reality-based attractions that can transport an audience
of 350 to another reality. Trumbull regards Luxor as "an
experiment in finally going over the edge of a belief barrier
through careful control of photography and projection, to
the point where a motion picture can be seen to be a real live
event."[1] In the words of Rheingold, "Trumbull is consciously
experimenting at the edge of the envelope of human ability
to assimilate media."[2]

Trumbull, says Rheingold, has had a long-standing desire
to go beyond the photo-realistic ideal of today's computer
artists and create perceptions that are even more fine-grained
than reality. If reality is 50 million polygons per second, as
computer graphics whiz Alvy Ray Smith has been quoted as
estimating, Trumbull wants 500 million.

Photo-real graphics are soon to come. And computer
visionaries other than Trumbull (Steve Jobs of Pixar, for
instance) boast they will make their virtual realms with more

pixel-depth than the actual surfaces our eyes see in the real world.

In the end, as described in the blockbuster futuristic movie *Total Recall,* where virtual reality has become fully state-of-the-art, "your brain won't know the difference."[3] At that point, seamless illusion will be as tangible and real as outward reality. Then people can really get lost in the maze of experience. It can be used to alter consciousness. Boundaries can be broken like never before. As God said in Genesis, "and now nothing will be restrained from them, which they have imagined to do" (Genesis 11:6 KJV). *What men imagine, they will be able to do.*

The Hardware

There are a variety of virtual reality systems currently in use, and new techniques are being devised all the time. The most basic system uses a conventional computer as a window through which a person can view the virtual world. More convincing systems use specialized hardware to create an "immersive" experience. A simple version of the immersive technology uses several large display screens to build the experience around the user. Glove interface devices also fit into this environment, though they tend to limit the freedom that is built in this atmosphere.

"Telepresence" is a form of virtual reality that connects the user of the system to remote sensors in some part of the real world. Surgeons who use tiny cameras to see inside patients for the most nonintrusive kinds of surgery are a current model for this kind of activity. So are on-the-street cameras that allow users to see, talk to, and eventually even touch real people in another location. But full-bore immersive systems are far more complex and will be described below. They are the classic virtual reality outfit.

A spate of new movies such as *Virtuosity* and *Lawnmower Man* have portrayed the full outfit—a computer and wires attached to someone wearing a full-body outfit that resembles a space suit in something like an operating theater. Participants can stand or sit. In most cases, the virtual reality outfit consists of a head-mounted display (usually a helmet with goggles), data gloves, and sometimes force-feedback armatures.

At present, there are problems with immersive body gear. It is still cumbersome and distracting. The real trouble is that present helmets with viewing screens do not work the way the real world does. Two video displays (one for each eye) with parallax are not exactly what your eyes are used to seeing. At the least, they cause eyestrain (imagine being a few inches from a TV set for several hours). Even more ominously, they can cause "binocular dysphoria," a defect in depth perception, for several hours after removing the head mount. Undoubtedly, bioengineering will overcome these obstacles.

Even considering the cumbersome body gear, current immersive virtual reality systems provide a realistic enough environment so that people training for high-risk jobs can use this technology to gain crucial experience without danger, such as the flight simulator. Nicholas Negroponte, director of Massachusetts Institute of Technology (M.I.T.) Media Lab, remarks that pilots can take the controls of fully loaded passenger planes for their first flights because they have learned more in the flight simulator than they could in a real plane. In the simulator, a pilot can be subjected to rare situations that, in the real world, could be deadly—for example, going into a spin, a stall, or a free fall. Thus he learns how to react in a situation where a wrong reaction could be lethal. Both a human life and an expensive plane are saved.

David Kupelian, of Chancellor Broadcasting, reports that the U.S. Defense Department is now using a virtual reality training program called SIMNET to train helicopter pilots. In use at military installations nationwide, it simulates a variety of battles including the Persian Gulf War. In other applications, architects can walk clients through a virtual building. Architectural modeling systems allow new home buyers to see what their as-yet-unbuilt houses will look like from the inside. Surgeons can practice operations on virtual bodies from a distance. The Boston Computer Museum has a virtual reality exhibit on cellular biology. And there is now a high school math program that uses virtual reality for visual representation of calculus equations. By the year 2001 virtual reality is projected to be a $4.5 billion industry.[4]

Digital Engines and Simulated Realities

The stunning and lifelike dinosaurs in *Jurassic Park* were created by computer animation at George Lucas's Industrial Light and Magic studios in Marin County, California. By contrast, Walt Disney's *Fantasia*, the greatest of all animated films of yesteryear, was completely composed by teams of human artists and shot frame-by-frame on film. None of it took place inside a computer. In the most spectacular digitally enhanced movies such as *Total Recall, Terminator 2, Apollo 13, Casper*, and *Jurassic Park*, the computer illusions ranged from six minutes in *Jurassic Park* to 40 minutes in *Casper*. But what put a 1996 film entitled *Toy Story* in a whole new league is that *all of it is virtual.*[5]

A computer animation company near Berkeley called Pixar Productions has shown audiences exactly how effectively computers can generate alternate realities. Pixar's *Toy Story* is the first major film ever made *without* human actors, props, cameras, or physical locations of any kind. The film was born in cyberspace as Pixar's bank of 300 Sun processors rendered the movie into its final form as massive amounts of digital information determined the animation, shifting perspective, shading, and lighting. The only human element present was the human voices dubbed into the talking animations. Even those could have been synthesized by computer, except the effect would have been too alien to appeal to the sentiments of present audiences.

Toy Story won over audiences with a certain mechanical charm through the "personalities" of its computer-generated talking toys. Perhaps that is more scary than it sounds. Audiences were able to participate in a movie fantasy of sounds and sights coming directly from the digital realm in a seamless computer-generated fantasy world.

If you want to picture what fully operational virtual reality is like—which is not quite here yet—just think of yourself thrust interactively into *Toy Story* as one of the characters. You are the size of the other toys and you can now talk to the space ranger, Buzz Lightyear, or Cowboy Woody while you "see" on their three-dimensional plane. You can see, hear, smell, and feel things within the perspectives and confines of that world. You also have the ability to act, and your actions create direct cause and effect, rippling out to ten million permutations, like a stone skipping in a giant pond. If you scream at the various talking toys from the bed, they will all respond in individual ways. Some might grimace, some might choose to ignore you. You can even push the space ranger out the window, as Cowboy Woody did, and hear him scream as you watch him fall in three-dimensional simulated space and then bounce near the drainpipe and into the bushes. As you push him through the window, you can feel it with your hands and body. You are fully there in the virtual realm. To pull this off takes immense computer power and a man-machine interface that we do not have yet. Digital technology is still working on the visual gateway. And that aspect of virtual reality is creeping into more and more movies, replacing expensive sets.

As things stand, computer-generated virtual-reality landscapes in live interactive sessions still have a cartoonish and ghostly appearance. Silicon Graphics in Mountain View, California offers a graphics supercomputer—called the RealityEngine2—that can render two million polygons per second under ideal conditions, which is less than two percent of the speed needed for verisimilitude.* We perceive the real world at more than 50 million polygons per second. "If you want photorealism, then for many environments, a RealityEngine2 is

---

*The quality or state of being realistic.

woefully inadequate," states Joshua Larson-Mogal of the Advanced Graphics Division at Silicon Graphics. "But while realism may have something to do with virtual reality, it is not a necessary condition by any means."[6]

There are other limitations as well. As Wayt Gibb reports in the *Scientific American,*

> Fooling a human brain into believing it is somewhere it is not is a tricky task. So far most research has focused on deceiving the eyes. High-resolution, wide-angle, three-dimensional displays are one obvious prerequisite; devices that track the direction of your gaze are another. Yet current virtual reality helmets that place a miniature liquid-crystal screen in front of each eye are grainy and expensive. The military spends up to $1 million each for the best, which offer the resolution of a typical desktop computer monitor—viewed at a distance of about four inches.[7]

A World of 20,000 Polygons

When I attended a worldwide premier of virtual reality at Club DV8 for a selected audience, put on by Spectrum HoloByte in San Francisco in a state-of-the-art exhibit for December 1991, what I experienced was a virtual landscape that was disappointingly wispy and crude. It was a world with objects made out of transparent tissue paper, atoms and pixels of far less density than the actual world.

My guess is that I was seeing less than 20,000 polygons per second—a mere fraction of what a RealityEngine2 computer produces, which itself is less than two percent of perceived visual reality. I found the cartoonesque landscape far too simple to be fully engaging. The primary colors and simple geometrical structures were not really what I had expected. And physically pivoting, with a heavy helmet on, attached to wires and hoses, was awkward and constraining.

Each attendee was invited to participate in a four-player game called "Dactyl Nightmare." Players stood on an elevated platform, blind to onlookers, with helmets on, virtual gloves, and holding cable-gun joysticks. Each participant would pivot in various directions while squeezing buttons and spasmodically pointing cable-gun joysticks. They were, in fact, shooting at each other and trying to escape flying pteredactyls. To me the first irony was that the theme of the debut of virtual reality was a death game in an imaginary realm of horrors. I sensed this would set the tenor for things to come. This was the first among what would be the next generation of video arcade games—*virtual* arcade games.

If I had to choose a metaphor, I would say the participants looked like *insect* pupae, each standing in the darkness with a full-fitting arachnid helmet and body gear attached to various black hoses and wires coming out of the elevated cages. On the surface, the whole thing looked antinatural and alien. At the time, I noted to myself, and later repeated in a radio interview about the future of virtual reality, "Say little Johnny is at a video arcade some years hence and feeds into a scanner the yearbook picture of his fifth-grade teacher who just reprimanded him. What he does with her in the fields of virtual reality is up to him. He might start by shooting her. Later he might put her in the middle of the Tower of London or a voodoo ceremony, and so on. Johnny—immune from cause and effect on this virtual plane—could slowly grow strange new tastes along the lines of serial killer James Bundy." It is a perfect doorway to dehumanizing others.

If taste in video arcade games is any indication, virtual games, such as the ever popular "Mortal Kombat" or "Doom," will be just as dark. They could propel the minds of new generations of youth to strange new places. The moral ceiling of these games will be no higher than the cyber-mind-set of those who put together most of the world's network and entertainment technology in the San Francisco Bay Area— from Silicon Valley, Palo Alto, Menlo Park, San Francisco, Marin County, to Berkeley. By default, they are the youth's tutors through their sophisticated games. These games do much more than just entertain as they explore the occult, sex, and violence above all. If you need to be convinced, go out and buy some of the top-selling video games like "Doom." One CD-ROM game even involves hunt and rape. What is the moral level of the cyber-culture that is setting the cutting-edge pace of video—and soon virtual reality—games?

Wired editor Eric Davis wrote an article about technopagans, citing Bay area cyber-whiz Mark Pesce as a case in point. Pesce is an M.I.T. dropout who practices witchcraft and coordinates a Bay area coven of fellow software and hardware cutting-edge innovators. He describes himself as a "gay witch." He does not write games per se, but is doing much more. He is creating a major cyberspace doorway that would have the power to allow global game-playing in three dimensions among international participants—games of all varieties, such as cyber-Dungeons and Dragons. Davis comments,

> Sure, he spends his time practicing kundalini yoga, boning up on Aleister Crowley's Thelemic magic, and tapping away at his book *Understanding Media: The End of Man*, which argues that magic will play a key role in combating the virulent information memes and pathological virtual worlds that will plague the coming cyberworld. But he's also the creator of VRML, a technical standard for creating navigable, hyperlinked 3-D spaces on the World Wide Web. . . . As Pesce's technomagical children, WorldView and VRML may well end up catalyzing the next phase of online mutation: the construction of a true, straight-out-of-*Neuromancer* cyberspace on the Internet.[8]

Davis then makes a telling remark about the technopagan cyber-culture in general:

> If you hang around the San Francisco Bay area or the Internet fringe for long, you'll hear loads of loopy talk about computers and consciousness. Because the issues of interface design, network psychology, and virtual reality are so open-ended and novel, the people who hack this conceptual edge often sound as much like science fiction acidheads as they do sober programmers. In this vague realm of

gurus and visionaries, technopagan ideas about "myth" and
"magic" often signify dangerously murky waters.[9]

"Your Brain Will Not Know the Difference"

In the futuristic blockbuster about virtual reality, *Total
Recall*, starring Arnold Schwarzenegger, the science of virtual
reality has evolved from all the burdensome external body
gear to a direct computer hookup at the neurological gateway
of the five senses—right inside the brain. Instead of a crude
electrode interface to nerve endings, an enormously powerful
computer chip—a *bio* chip—is implanted. Now the visual,
auditory, and tactile centers are reached directly and respond
at their full range. It produces a level of virtual reality that
equals, if not surpasses, reality.

In *Total Recall*, virtual reality has become a commercial
enterprise among competing high-tech corporations who
guarantee the ultimate vacation or thrill of a lifetime, cheaply.
It all happens inside the brain and the brain cannot tell the
difference. The virtual package also custom-tailors the experience for individual personal tastes—in this case, Doug
Quaid's tastes, played by Schwarzenegger:

> "Now let me see. The basic Mars package will run you 899
> credits," said the salesman for RECALL Inc. "Now that's for two
> full weeks of memories, complete in every detail. If you want a
> longer trip that'll cost you a little more, because it's a deeper
> implant."

> "What's in the two-week package?" asks Quaid.

> RECALL salesman: "First of all, Doug, let me tell you. When you
> go RECALL you get nothing but first class memories. Private
> cabin on the Shuttle, Deluxe suite at the Hilton, plus all the
> major sights—Mount Pyramid, the Grand Canals, and of course,
> Venusville!"

> Quaid: "But how real does it seem?"

> RECALL salesman: "As real as any memory in your head."

Quaid: "Come on, don't BS me."

RECALL salesman: "No, I'm telling you, Doug, your brain will not know the difference. . . . When you travel with RECALL, everything is perfect. So what do you say?"

Quaid even has the option of customizing a virtual woman for his individual tastes:

RECALL doctor: "How do you like your women? Blonde, brunette, redhead?"

Quaid: "Brunette."

RECALL doctor: "Slim, athletic, voluptuous?"

Quaid: "Athletic."

RECALL doctor: "Demure, aggressive, sleazy?"

Quaid: "Sleazy . . . and demure."

RECALL doctor to technician: "41A, Ernie."

Ernie: "Oh boy, is he going to have a wild time. He's not gonna want to come back!"[10]

Entertainment and mind control have less than two degrees of separation in *Total Recall*. They are virtually the same thing. The film engrosses the audience in a massive plot of intrigue revolving around a corporate colony on Mars. *Recall*'s entertainment package lives up to its billing . . . or, *was it all real?* Did Quaid's force of will overcome the implant, or did the implant uncover hidden areas of his brain blocked out by a CIA-level program going back to a prior identity of Quaid as a high-level agent? Or . . . is that memory part of the virtual chip? You get the point. We are on a balance beam trying to interpret what is going on as the movie rockets along from intrigue to violent encounter.

The point of the film is that they have balanced things down to the last detail. Evidence is divided down the middle for either interpretation. Either the whole incredible drama was a virtual reality experience, or it all really happened. To quote RECALL, Inc., "Your mind does not know the difference." And this goes for the audience looking at the film as well as Quaid.

What this virtual reality fiction brings up is the question of what happens to a mind once invaded with an alternate reality as real as the outward world. Or can this technology be used as a weapon for mind control? Or, in the Huxley sense, can it finally bring entertainment and mind control together?

What lures people to go through these doors of experience is the constant quest for knowledge, power, and expansion of abilities. At the seat of the quest for mind expansion is the seeming capacity, in altered consciousness, to find heightened abilities, godlike powers, and universal knowledge.

Altered Consciousness

Cyber-culture has pondered the following combination.

The first stage: Take the human mind and hook it up to what will someday become fully functional virtual reality, the seamless illusion at full thrust invading all the doors of perception—visually at more than 50 million polygons per second, audibly by holographic surround-sound, plus full-body sensing and tactile gear, and maybe even smells thrown in as well.

Now, the booster rocket: Take the subject's mind while hooked up to virtual reality and manipulate it directly, either with a range of powerful psychochemicals, such as LSD, or by hypnosis. Keep in mind that under LSD alone just gazing at a flower can rocket the subject off to other worlds. What happens if that same person on LSD were to enter fully charged virtual reality? Could it amplify the psychedelic experience an entire order of magnitude—the very catalyst the 60s generation has longed for—to a new kind of critical mass of consciousness? These are questions the cyber-culture—already into designer and smart drugs—has been asking for a long time.

If someone under deep hypnosis were hooked up to full-bore virtual reality, could that person enter a doorway opening up psychic powers? If the virtual reality program itself fully simulated psychic or occult experience, such as astral projection, remote viewing, or contact with spirit beings, could that catalyze a genuine mediumistic experience? And would this not especially apply to someone who had a mediumistic family history? As David Kupelian remarks, "To be totally immersed in a computer-generated 3-D environment that results in the suspension of one's normal sensibilities is perhaps *the* technological two-edged sword of the future."[11]

In *The Other Side of Death,* I reported that the hypnotic trance state was the critical factor that opened up most psychics and mediums in the first place. Suddenly they had various powers and could sense familiar spirits. After Edgar Cayce learned to self-induce a trance, he became much more psychic than when he was simply lucid dreaming. Cayce travelled out of the body, met spirit guides or "entities," and gave life readings. The breakthrough happened when a famous Jewish theosophist in Chicago paid Cayce to be hypnotized and asked him ultimate questions about reincarnation and soul evolution. Suddenly the man who looked like a Baptist school teacher became a New Ager. When Cayce went under, it was as though something else took over. After that, his notoriety grew quickly and he was able to go from "medical readings" to "life readings."

It is a fact that most mediums *became* mediums in the first place by undergoing hypnosis and then accessing realms that the Bible plainly warns against. Mediums usually learn to self-induce trances as part of their craft. In the same way, subjects under today's modern hypnotherapists increasingly report past-life recall or UFO encounters. *The key thing is the trance.*

How deeply can the mind be penetrated when it is not only hooked up to computer-generated virtual reality but when it is further opened up by hypnosis or psychotropic drugs? Sense-experience fanatics of this generation will no doubt combine drugs to enhance their virtual reality trips. It will be the next great thing, the thing to surpass LSD in the same way that acid broke the ceiling of experience in the 1960s, if you will, occultizing the mind. It will also be perhaps another quantum leap in occultizing American culture, perhaps as much as acid did in the 1960s.

Virtual Gods

Like all powers, there is a dark side to this quest for mind expansion and virtual entertainment. "Virtual lab" is a dead giveaway. It is also a metaphor. To enter virtual reality, people must first abandon the real world, like ghosts, and descend into a darkened chamber to stare into a realm created out of artificial light. It will never be as bright as the noonday sun. And the tastes it feeds will never rise to those aesthetic levels of sheer beauty that nature can satisfy in the middle of spring in myriad settings across the globe. Virtual tastes will rise to no greater level than that provided by those who feed the machine, both the thrill-seekers and software and cyber engineers. Its moral ceiling will go no higher than the dim light of an underground world.

As man creates his own book of Genesis, his creation will ultimately grow dark and turn on him, much like Frankenstein turned on its own master in that famous novel written in the last century. Whether or not there is a "ghost in the machine" with some kind of supernatural interface, the entertainment aspect alone can turn ghosts out of its viewers as they escape to simulated worlds, leaving family and friends behind. Then more baseball gloves will hang in the basement along with picnics, walks in the park, drives through the country, and a thousand other activities in the real world, activities that make life rich and bring people together in real intimacy. In virtual worlds, other hungers are fed and exchanged for activities in the real world. You can read about some of these hungers in the ancient accounts of Sodom and

Gomorrah. They were real then and they are becoming real again now. *Sin recruits through corruption.*

When the doorway to seduction goes from being a trap-door to a city gate, offering a full flood of experiences, then recruitment grows small numbers to hoards. That is how cultures change. It happened in Rome and it happened in Sodom and Gomorrah. Another way to describe change is *decay* and *corruption.* When that happens, cultures are destroyed through the momentum of their folly when their actions bring back thunderous consequences. That is the human side of the momentum of God's judgment.

Let's discuss corruption within the human soul by looking at the slag heap of recent history. Part of the delusion of our time is to minimize evil and deny that people can be so evil. What kind of thoughts do you think serial murderer and pedophile John Wayne Gayce had? Thirty decomposed bodies were buried under and around his house. Most had been tortured. What kind of thoughts do you think homosexual serial killer Jeffrey Dahmer had? In his case, some of the decomposing bodies were in his icebox—bodies sexually assaulted, murdered, some of them even eaten. I will spare you the horrific details of both cases. For most of us, this terrain is far too alien to plumb. It is mean stuff. My point is, though, that when the Bible uses the word *vile* or *abomination* it does so for a purpose. Such things exist in our culture and they exist in our history books and *God warns about it.* Evil has a way of spreading. That was the point of recounting the example of Sodom and Gomorrah.

How much more quickly would today's youth corruption increase if, somewhere in the middle of the technopagan culture of software geniuses, several came along with the inner landscape of a Jeffrey Dahmer or a John Wayne Gayce? They would have the power to create the software entertainment for millions of youth. That is quite a pipeline into a culture. They could push the envelope of accepted thinking here and bend it there. They would be playing their own private video game with a whole live culture. And the moguls of Hollywood, seeing a profit, would not stand in their way, but in defense would cry "censorship" to narrow-minded protestations from the "religious right." And adults who were oblivious to the high-tech youth culture would not have a clue what was going on. Of course, this is a hypothetical example.

Will virtual reality be any more virtuous as entertainment than its predecessors in the movie, television, cable TV, and interactive CD-ROM industries? Will it raise us to new heights of moral purity and virtue, restoring our lost national innocence? Only someone very naive and dull, I think, would answer yes at this point in history. Virtual entertainment will continue to steer us—apart from an act of God—toward the spiritual landscape that existed before the last great judgment when imaginations before the great deluge dwelt only on evil day in and day out. The doorway is the imagination. To repeat an earlier observation, virtual reality intersects human vulnerability where desires and longings meet the imagination. And that makes it a formidable mind-machine. With it, man will spin new webs.

As man creates his universe with no other gods in it but himself, his creation will ultimately grow dark. The human creator who himself is long estranged from his Creator, the Living God, will now try to play God as he creates alternative realities. Virtual realities can never be more than either a poor mirror of the actual reality that God created, thus borrowing from whatever is already in existence, or they will simply be mutations and perversions of these previously created things.

> And they said, Go to, let us build us a city and a tower, whose top may reach unto heaven; and let us make us a name, lest we be scattered abroad upon the face of the whole earth.
>
> And the LORD came down to see the city and the tower, which the children of men builded.

And the LORD said, Behold, the people is one, and they
have all one language; and this they begin to do: and now
nothing will be restrained from them, which they have
imagined to do (Genesis 11:4-6 KJV).

6

VIRTUAL BODIES IN THE CITY OF BITS

Donald L. Baker

OVERVIEW

Donald Baker takes us into the digital sea of cyberspace to help us understand the forces shaping and bending this emerging electronic society that hovers over the earth and its national boundaries. It swims with all sorts of beliefs. There are hybrids of political correctness tied to neopagan notions forming new norms. There is the infestation of postmodern beliefs in endless invisible (electronic) conference rooms. For the millions entering this unchartered sea, especially cyber-youth, their minds and beliefs are out there for the picking, to be gathered and trimmed by those controlling the predominant modes of belief. There are black holes and eddies lying deep within the folds of cyberspace poised to attract straying net-surfers. Some open the gateway to witch-craft and others into gender-bending experiments. At the same time, there are endless legitimate sites that can tell you almost anything—from the price of a four-year-old Mercedes Benz in Bonn, to the weather in Cairo, to how to get discount tickets for theaters around Shaftesbury Avenue in London. How do we navigate this maze? is the oft-asked question.

Cyberspace, we are often told, is a disembodied medium.
Testimonies to this effect are everywhere. . . . In a sense,
these testimonies are correct; the body remains in front of
the screen rather than within it. In another sense, however,
they are deeply misleading, for they obscure the crucial role
that the body plays in constructing cyberspace. In fact, we
are never disembodied.
—N. Katherine Hayle
Immersed in Technology: Art and
Virtual Environments[1]

n chapter 2, I discussed two hidden building
blocks of cyberspace—two mythic concepts whose proponents are currently engaged in a Darwinian struggle for cyber-
cultural dominance. The first posits an electronic frontier, a
wide-open digital vista in which cyber-citizens are allowed
total freedom to communicate and share files without "real-
life" government control or community-imposed restrictions.
The second model imagines cyberspace as a place of control,
a place where massive quantities of data are manipulated and

made useful through helpful software programs (including virtual reality), and where children are protected from obscene on-line material through similarly helpful software filters. The telecommunications reform bill enacted in 1996 leans to this second model, assigning Internet service providers the task of policing their networks to prevent the availability of obscene content.

Commenting on this model, Michael Sorkin notes that in cyberspace, "the body, the person, no longer simply exists in public space but actually becomes it. . . . "[2] And virtual reality only exacerbates the potential loss of privacy, according to art and robotics professor, Simon Penny:

> The prospect of real-time surveillance is so much more simply facilitated in virtual reality: not only will the computer know where you are, but what kind of information you are accessing and where your various body parts are at the time. As digital media become ever-more encapsulating, so the possibility of permanent real-time surveillance becomes real.[3]

Our growing fear of physical monitoring and surveillance in cyberspace is but one aspect of cyber-millennial anxieties relating to our physical bodies. What are the sources of this anxiety?

The Body in Question

The adoption (in Europe and America) of the 18th-century Enlightenment belief in reason over faith, and the similarly man-imposed cleft between materiality and spirituality, are at the root of the problem. Loss of faith in a transcendent God and, by extension, belief in the inherent dignity of the human body are the result.

God created man in His image, and we are intended to fulfill that function in our whole being. Brian J. Walsh and J. Richard Middleton comment:

> Human beings are God's ambassadors, his representatives, to the rest of creation. We are the stewards he has set in

authority over the earth to manifest his presence and to reflect his glory in all our cultural doings.

But note that the image consists in our bodily representation of God. The whole person, and not some inner spiritual part, is created in God's image. We reflect God's glory and represent him on earth by our total, physical presence. Indeed, visibility is of the essence, for we are to make the invisible God visible by our lives.[4]

In losing faith in the God of the Bible, Western culture kicked out the support for understanding man (*in the body*) as God's representation on earth. Also lost was the truth that the body of every redeemed believer is a temple of the Holy Spirit (1 Corinthians 6:19). A corresponding desire for a secular utopia romanticized the role of machines, notably in artists' movements prior to the mechanized slaughter of World War I:

The Futurists, such as Marinetti and Malevich, saw in the machine the energy and strength sufficient for the construction of utopian societies. For cubist painters, human beings began to resemble complex mechanisms. Artists such as Leger, Feininger, Kandinsky, and Picasso began to fill the visual landscape with robotlike creatures.[5]

Beginning with the Great War, the experiences of the 20th century have provided one body blow after another to the culture. More humans have been killed and mutilated in our century—in more various and horrific ways—than ever before. Marxism-Leninism and Fascism in particular—the most utopian of modern philosophies—seem to have held the greatest hatred for the body, even as they denied an otherworldly existence.

Advanced technology has been deployed for much of this century's grim-reaping. Then, too, first machinery and now computers have been responsible for the loss of millions of jobs in the name of efficiency, even as many more jobs have been created by the new technologies. Industrialization—and now computerization (also known by its euphemism, postindustrialization)—has occurred so rapidly that we have had insufficient time to adapt to the existence of machines in our landscape, and to their effects on our lives. (In the U.S. only the Amish, who I mentioned in chapter 2 as living in "principled cultural irrelevancy," have made the decision to accept new technology at their own pace, and in their own ways.)

Pop culture has repeatedly mirrored our anxiety over our relationship with machines—from Charlie Chaplin's struggle with ruthless metal gears in *Modern Times*, to the unstoppable man-machine hybrids, the Borg, in "Star Trek—The Next Generation." Cultural critics Arthur and Marilouise Kroker contend that the media are offering us images they call "panic bodies" that reflect all the grisly symptoms of culture burnout:

> The hysteria around physical fitness, civil liberties, AIDS treatment, the right to life, the right to death, eating disorders, the war on drugs, surveillance in the workplace, steroids in pro sports, and the sexual exploits of public figures are all symptoms [of panic bodies].[6]

Multimedia artist and writer Nell Tenhaaf draws on Freudian psychoanalytic theory to suggest that our current fixation with cyberspace may be "a 'hysterical' fantasy of the late twentieth century...expressing an inutterable [sic] desire for a more fluid subjectivity and a body that knows itself better, and this by a simulation through technologies of enhanced organic behavior [that is, a wired-up body]."[7]

According to the postmodern philosophy popular in the current cyber-millennial period, the body is tainted by its inescapable connection with sex-based gender, and thereby with sexual politics—particularly the perceived white-male domination of women and the non-Western world. The following statement, from a Canadian (male) professor, is typical:

> Men's fascination with technology is linked to the masculine need to be in control of the material world, to know how to extend that control, to be able to act, and to be

independent of reliance on others. In this respect science and technology are dominantly male in nature and have been forged from the development of capitalism, materialism, and individualism in western culture since the Renaissance. Reason is the supporting structure of the masculine fascination with technology and its products.[8]

Postmodern philosophy views the body as the locus of a continuing battleground for political and sexual power. Kathy Acker, a feminist author, was asked: "Your books always return to the site of the body: as a source of power, a center of struggle for power, as the place we finally exist in, as opposed to our thoughts. Why generally are you so interested in the body?" Her answer is enlightening:

> When reality—the meanings associated with reality—is up for grabs—which is certainly . . . one of the central problems in philosophy and art ever since the end of the 19th century—then the body itself becomes the only thing you can return to. . . . It's the body which finally can't be touched by all our skepticism and ambiguous systems of belief. The body is the only place where any basis for real values exists anymore.[9]

The Body Inadequate?

Kathy Acker, Neil Tenhaaf, and Arthur and Marilouise Kroker are responding, in their own ways, to the relentless assault of science, technology, and postmodern culture upon our self-concept. Our society is rendering the body obsolete through the technologies of communication and calculation, which mock our physical limitations. At the same time, the processes of postindustrialization and urbanization, and the breakdown in morality derived from the "death" of God, have alienated us from each other, increasing the natural fear and distrust we have of those we perceive as outsiders.

Postmodernism teaches that reality is socially constructed—not objectively factual—and that language is a tool used by the powerful to control others. "According to the postmodernists," notes Gene Edward Veith, "all reality is virtual reality. We are all wearing helmets that project our own separate little worlds. We can experience these worlds and lose ourselves in them, but they are not real, nor is one person's world exactly the same as someone else's. We are not creating our own reality, however. Rather, we accept a reality made by someone else."[10] Therefore, it seems logical that our bodies are the only refuge left to us. Yet, even the body is not a safe haven, for we are all subject to detection, surveillance, and penetration by an increasing number of technological devices.

As a result, many today seem to harbor a secret inner wish to leave the flesh behind, to project their consciousness into the cyberspace of TV, computer networks, and virtual reality. Rejecting transcendence through traditional Western religious practices, many in our culture are desperately seeking a gnostic release from the body. They seek this release in a number of ways—through orgiastic sensory experience, Eastern religious experiences, and escape into cyberspace.

There are some, however, who are desperate, not because they hate the body, or seek safety in it, but because they see it as inadequate to participate in the possibilities available to the mind in the cyber-millennium: the comprehension and manipulation of electronic data directly through the brain; the augmentation or substitution of body parts with manufactured replacements or prosthetic devices; the possibility of life extension—even "immortality"—through the transfer of consciousness to computers. The body is imagined, to be blunt, *as obsolete*—no longer worthy of the psalmist's praise (Psalm 139:13-14).

The Australian performance artist, Stelarc, makes his living by demonstrating the body's need for technological augmentation. He fabricates and straps on a variety of electromechanical devices to his body, manipulating them for his audience. He has even inserted a camera into his stomach to videotape his interior. Though Stelarc asserts he is only an artist, not a scientist, NASA engineers have been impressed enough with his skills to examine his robotic "third arm." Here are some of Stelarc's ruminations on obsolescence:

> It is time to question whether a bipedal, breathing, beating body with binocular vision and a 1400cc brain is now an adequate biological form. The human species has created a technological and information environment it can no longer cope with. . . . Distraught and disconnected, the body can only resort to interface and symbiosis. The body may not yet surrender its autonomy, but certainly its mobility. Plugged into a machine network, the body needs to be pacified. In fact, to function in the future and to truly achieve a HYBRID SYMBIOSIS, the body will need to become increasingly anesthetized.[11]

The perceived need for a "hybrid symbiosis" has permeated academia. Carnegie Mellon robotics professor Hans Moravec is perhaps the best-known supporter. In his book *Mind Children*, Moravec advocates the development of technology that, one day in the not-too-distant future, will be capable of "downloading" one's very consciousness from the physical brain into a computer, thence becoming a silicon-based life-form. As Katherine Hayles points out, "it is apparent that Moravec equates subjectivity with the mind. The body is treated as a flawed and unwieldy vehicle, necessary in the early stages of human evolution but now become more trouble than it is worth . . . a superfluous accessory."[12]

This attitude has been graphically developed in the cyberpunk science fiction novels of the 1980s and early 1990s. In William Gibson's *Neuromancer* series, freelance "deck cowboys" named Case and Count Zero project themselves into a worldwide virtual-reality cyberspace called the Matrix, from which they steal computer data for corporate clients. While not "jacked-in," the hackers suffer the indignity of entrapment in the flesh, or "meat," and prowl an international street-culture where designer-drug addiction and bionic implants are commonplace.

What makes reading cyberpunk so unsettling—besides the characters' foul mouths—is realizing that Gibson and his colleagues have simply extrapolated current technology trends into the future. In the cyber-millennium, it will soon become easy to connect all sorts of personal electronic devices—cell phone, Walkman, medical monitoring system, global positioning system, pacemaker, and so forth—into an integrated body-net linked wirelessly to the Internet. As we age or encounter disease and accidents, more microelectronic and inorganic replacement parts will become available to repair—*even augment*—our failing bodies. More surgery will be performed by computer-guided, robotic surgeons whose "hands" will prove far steadier than the finest surgeon's (who will be relegated to operating the keyboard or joystick). At what point in the 21st century will we—or our children—admit we have actually become cyborgs, experiencing what postmoderns call "boundary problems"?[13]

Polymorphous Perversity and Cyberspace

Virtual reality and other cyberspace experiences have, especially in cyberpunk fiction, been regarded hopefully as the means of collapsing boundaries between the body and the overwhelming amount of data generated by advanced information systems. But the prospect and reality of cyberspace-induced boundary-collapse excites many academics, and not because they want to demystify the datacloud. Rather, they are looking to cyberspace as a laboratory for advancing theories of gender-based sexuality.

I noted earlier that the body has become a battleground for neo-Marxist, postmodern proponents eager to bring to an end what they see as the power-mongering patriarchy inherited from Western ("Christian") culture. This patriarchy, woven into our concepts of reality and language, is considered responsible for continuing oppression of minority groups in general and women in particular. Overthrowing

Western cultural institutions, beliefs, and legal structures will, they believe, eliminate oppression.

So where does cyberspace (virtual reality) fit in? It is the malleability of cyberspace that is exciting to radical postmodernism fans, in that persons interacting in cyberspace can adopt their own personas, and have the freedom (except on company time, of course) to change anything about themselves they want: name, age, sex, personality—in short, they can lie without suffering face-to-face consequences. Cyberspace appears to allow one to escape the controls imposed by the patriarchal culture—to collapse the boundaries between *the actual* and *the desirable*. Future multimedia and virtual reality software will permit even more radical alterations in reality's perception to the point where one may be able to adopt any appearance desired, and to interact not only with other persons, but even with programmed ideas and concepts that may exhibit more interesting behavior than real people express in real life.[14]

The guiding postmodern principle here is that personality is not fixed, but is—like reality—a social construct. Neo-Marxist, radical feminists take this idea one step further, and decouple the concept of gender from physical sexuality. Thus, gender is not a given, they claim, but "polymorphous perversity"—a performance or learned behavior that need not be linked to physical sexuality.[15]

The technical term for this belief is gender feminism. It is an attempt to force society to accept not only the total equality of women with men, but also the total normality of homosexuality in all its variations, including transsexuality (the physical transformation, through surgery, of a person from one sex to the other) and transgenderism (to my understanding, the conscious choice of one's sexual identity, unrelated to one's possessing either male or female sex organs).

Gender feminists mounted a major international campaign for acceptance of their agenda at the Fourth World Conference on Women, held in Beijing in September 1995. In their pursuit of a radical restructuring of power between men and women on a global basis, gender feminists from the United States, Canada, and Europe largely ignored important developing-world women's issues, such as protecting the status of stay-at-home mothers and protecting families from religious persecution. Instead, the developed-world representatives, including former congresswoman Bella Abzug, pushed for 50-50 male-female quotas for all elected and appointed government positions, and called for abortion and sexual rights for lesbians and adolescents to be declared fundamental human rights.

A similar agenda was advanced in a smaller, but nonetheless influential, venue a year prior to the Beijing conference. Attenders at the Fourth International Conference on Cyberspace and the Art and Virtual Environment Symposium, held at Canada's Banff Centre for the Arts in May 1994, heard a number of speakers interpret cyberspace and virtual reality in overtly gender-feminist terms.[16] The most influential among these was conference organizer and self-styled "Goddess of Cyberspace," Allucquere Rosanne "Sandy" Stone, director of the Advanced Communication Technologies Laboratory at the University of Texas at Austin. Stone described Habitat, a Japanese virtual world with 1.5 million subscribers, which has since been brought to the United States as WorldsAway. A graphics-based on-line network, Habitat permits participants to choose male or female bodies (and human or animal heads) to represent themselves in the Habitat environment. Stone claimed that in Habitat, as well as in many other areas of cyberspace, the incidence of on-line "cross-dressing" is high. Men pose as women to attract attention, while women pretend to be men in order to avoid on-line creeps.[17]

Stone declared that her conscious goal is "getting at the power structures that maintain [gender bipolarity]" in a very real way. She performs this by deliberately placing the audience—*her students*—in a state of shock in order to introduce destabilizing ideas. Stone does this by showing slides of hermaphrodites, of people with mutilated bodies, such as war veterans with terrible wounds, and fakirs suspended by hooks through their flesh. After showing these slides to the attenders, she commented:

> When I show images like these to my students who are not sophisticated in the ways of art, I find that frequently they gasp. Their gasping tells me that a process has happened inside, some internal disruption. Something has interfered with their normal, seamless way of viewing the world. . . . And in that moment of interruption, when for just an instant the fabric of normality is ripped open a little bit, and they can see the nuts and bolts of the way reality is put together—if that moment can be encouraged and that rip teased further open, not just for them but for all of us, then perhaps we can get a handle on the nuts and bolts of reality and find ways to unscrew some of them. . . .
>
> These slides demonstrate aspects of the human form that we don't ordinarily see. Things that don't fit our accustomed structures of visual knowledge, our ways of perceiving shape or gender. When we think about the way that we normally see humans in the age of electronic communication, i.e. through some representational medium, they're being represented to us in terms of text, as strings of numbers or words turned into images. That is, they are not only visible, but legible, in the same way that texts are legible. And for that reason I refer to these kinds of disruptive images as being nearly legible, but not quite. There are different degrees of the legibility of the human body, and it's the boundary status of these images—shapes and genders that inhabit the boundaries between the accustomed and the utterly strange, the territory of the near-legible—that gives them their disruptive power. And the power of disruption is the power of change, the opportunity to see with new vision.[18]

One rarely hears such a radical agenda stated so plainly. Stone admits that her intent in showing images of bizarre behavior and extremely rare and unfortunate physical conditions is to disrupt her students' foundational beliefs about what is real, what is normative. Her goal is to influence others with gender-feminist ideas concerning self-concept and sexuality. Since most college students are in their late teens and early 20s—barely out of adolescence—Stone's strategy could be quite successful in destabilizing her students' deeply held, but unarticulated, beliefs about the nature and practice of sexual identity. More important, Stone is hardly a lone academic when she states, "The fact of the body changing is something I'm interested in promoting."[19]

Stone's description of her goals and methodology makes clear that the new world of digital cyberspace is not merely a place where people are trading files and searching for reference information. Cyberspace, like outer space, has become a new battleground in the sociopolitical struggles underway in the cyber-millennium. It is a place where the twin forces of technology and ideology chip away at the human frame, created by God with a glory and dignity that our society has largely forgotten.

It is crucial that we understand cyberspace as a place where we will spend increasing amounts of time, and get much useful work done. Since God created us as physical beings, however, *cyberspace can never be our home*. It will never be a place of escape from our body and its limitations, or from God. I agree with linguist George Lakoff when he muses:

> I could imagine some interesting and fun things to do with virtual reality and some important ones. . . . On the other hand, . . . the more you interact not with something natural and alive, but with something electronic, it takes the sense of the earth away from you, . . . robs you of more and more embodied experiences. That is a deep impoverishment of the human soul.[20]

7

EMBODY
THE AVATAR

John Moore

OVERVIEW

One of the hottest rages among the youth for more than a decade—interactive role-playing—has come on the Internet and it is creating an intoxicating cyber-world. At the moment, millions of net-surfers are speeding down the largest superhighway on the Internet to participate in this newly arrived imaginary realm constructed from virtual reality and various interactive games.

Fifteen years ago Dungeons and Dragons, the game that started this rage, took the nation by storm. It contained complex rules and long-term strategies seen in war-game theory used by the Pentagon. Instead of modern weapons being used, however, the players had magical powers and cast spells. Experience-hungry youth looking for an escape have become increasingly addicted to the alternate realms of these games.

Now with the advent of such games on the Internet—forming a kind of electronic astral plane—the population there will most likely soar. We need to ask in what direction the countless travelers who are choosing to live on the Internet will be taken as these realms become ever more exotic and powerful.

At first the scene is static: a featureless green plain stretches off into the distance, ending where it eventually meets a range of medium-sized mountains. These look a lot like the coastal range one might see driving down Highway 1 in California from the coastal area off Palo Alto to Santa Cruz. The scene is the same no matter which direction I face, except for the changing features of the mountains in the hazy distance. Now, suddenly, the green surface of the ground is beginning to roil—form and feature are beginning to appear.

I am "parachuting in" to AlphaWorld, a 140,000-square-mile tract of virtual landscape that recently appeared on the Internet. Now I can see that I am standing on the actual surface of AlphaWorld, at a spot designated "ground zero." This is the beginning of an AlphaWorld adventure.

In front of me I can see the "avatars" of several other recent arrivals. The other avatars—and this is an interesting term the software creators have used because it comes from only one source in the world, Hinduism, and has only one meaning, "incarnation of God"—are beginning to stumble across the virtual landscape. Each one responds to the movements of a "mouse" on a desktop somewhere, perhaps thousands of miles away from the computer that actually houses the bits and bytes of the plain upon which we are all standing. (To be fair, there are other labels in use, such as "agents," and "bots," but "avatar" is the reigning favorite and will likely drive the rest out.)

One avatar is communicating something to the other inhabitants of the world—a typed message above its head reads, "Help me . . . the teleport to the left of me is not working." It is a silent cry in a strange new world, and my avatar moves silently by, looking for clues in a land of unknowns. The irony of the situation is striking: the helpless cry of the "avatar"—this manifestation of a "god," overwhelmed and impotent—without a voice and without a friend on the plains of the new frontier.

Cyberspace is the new frontier of the imagination. And avatars are our first stumbling steps into the new world, the first pass at inhabiting this land of the mind and the machine. These avatars, however, are not just alter egos in a new techno-social matrix, they are also idols that exist on a virtual plane. Not formed of wood or stone—though grounded in silicon—they occupy a seamless digital plane. They are images of ourselves, of what we would like to be. And as the technology of virtual reality improves, they will increasingly become the images of what we dream we might become—the supermen, the avatars if you will, of the virtual world.

Virtual Dungeons and Dragons

AlphaWorld, and the various other avatar-based worlds that exist in cyberspace, represent the latest wave in man-machine interface. These worlds, also known as "habitats," allow a kind of social interaction to develop between the occupants. The roots of these worlds go back to the "MUD" (multi-user dungeon), which is the on-line version of multiplayer fantasy/role-playing adventure games such as Dungeons and Dragons. MUDs, which go back at least to the 1970s, have flourished on the Net, with player communities growing up around college and university computing networks.

Essentially, MUDs and their variants (MUSHs, MOOs, Tiny MUDs, and so forth) are text-based neighborhoods of cyberspace. For those unfamiliar with these Internet-based games, a MUD (multiuser dungeon) is a combat-oriented environment and the goal is often to build up your character by combating monsters. A MOO (multiuser object-oriented environment) is typically more socially oriented, allowing you to create your own rooms and objects. There are also MUSHs (multiuser shared hallucinations) and MUCKs (no meaning known) that are more difficult to define and tend toward the bizarre. Users interact with the multiuser dungeon environment and with each other by typing and receiving messages. Consider the following interaction between a player (P) and a MUD:

P: Turn left.

MUD: You are looking at a closed door.

P: Open door.

MUD: The door will not open.

P: Use key.

MUD: The door swings open, revealing a long passageway lit by torches mounted on the wall every 30 feet.

The cyberspace here, such as it is, has been created by the designer of the multiuser dungeon; the actual images, smells, sounds, and textures of this landscape are left to the imagination of the player. To paraphrase Snow Crash author Neal Stephenson, in some ways text may be the most effective virtual reality that will ever be developed. Multiuser dungeons have been created almost completely from textual descriptions of characters, spells, weapons, monsters, wizards, enchantresses, villages, wilderness areas, and, of course, dungeons. The power of these fantasy/role-playing games to capture the imagination of participants is well documented—even to the point that the "reality" of the fantasy world can sometimes wash over into the player's real life, creating bizarre episodes.

In AlphaWorld, on the other hand, the backgrounds, buildings, trees, ground, sky, and so forth, of the virtual world are stored as graphics in the computer, and displayed in three dimensions on a user's display. The computer is also in charge of maintaining the visual representation of the player's avatar for the benefit of the other players on the system. The movement of an avatar is under the control of the player's mouse or keyboard. A player can change the way he appears to others by choosing from a gallery of prefabricated, but slightly less generic, avatars. Advanced players can import their own custom avatar images, enabling players to become, essentially, whatever they want to be. Of course, restrictions apply: when transferred to the virtual realm the creator (man) must assume the form of his virtual creation in order to interact with it; he must therefore become the "avatar."

LucasFilm Habitat

This graphical type of interface was first introduced in the 1980s in a virtual world known as LucasFilm Habitat—or simply "Habitat" (also known as "Club Caribe").[1] Habitat ran on an early on-line service known as QuantumLink (the parent company, Quantum Computer Services, later went on to create a highly visible and immensely successful on-line service—America Online). Since QuantumLink was primarily targeted at Commodore 64 computers—now vastly outdated—there were severe restrictions on the computing horsepower that could be used to create the interface to the Habitat world.[2] Consequently, the images and avatars of Habitat were two-dimensional and cartoonish. Nevertheless, in its prime Habitat hosted several thousand on-line gamers. Habitat succeeded in becoming what was generally agreed to be the first of its kind—an avatar-based virtual world (a "habitat," according to the creators of the original Habitat).

Habitat was no kid's toy. Underneath the simplistic exterior, a serious experiment in "social computing" interface was underway. It was an experiment in creating a "very large scale commercial multi-user virtual environment."[3] Habitat eventually migrated to Japan as the "Fujitsu Habitat," then returned to the United States in an upgraded form as WorldsAway—now available on CompuServe. WorldsAway and AlphaWorld are just two of the many avatar-based worlds currently open for business on the Net. The creators of the original Habitat project, Chip Morningstar, and F. Randall Farmer have gone on to become key players in a new venture called "Electric Communities" (see Appendix B).

Ground Zero

While widespread distributed computing continues to revolutionize both business and personal life, the full benefits of this communications revolution will not be realized without a system that encompasses the *full richness of human interaction.*[4] (From the Electric Communities Web site, emphasis added)

Every technological advance must start somewhere. Powered flight began at Kitty Hawk, and today we have space shuttles and fleets of commercial jets ready to take travelers to destinations anywhere in the world. We are now witnessing the infancy of avatar-based virtual reality, but already the shape of the future is taking form. In AlphaWorld's less ambitious but more developed predecessor, WorldsChat, users browse through the avatar gallery, searching for that appropriate on-line alter ego. The avatars are presented as a series of framed pictures, hung in a gallery somewhere in cyberspace. As you stroll through the gallery, if you find an avatar that looks interesting, you can simply click on the picture for a demonstration of what the avatar looks like in action. The avatar springs to life; now it is out of the frame and resident in three-dimensional cyberspace. It turns around so you can see it from all sides: *Is this the cyber-body you would like to use to present yourself to others?* If so, click the "Embody Me" button; congratulations, you have a new persona. If not, simply click "Keep Looking"; the avatar returns to its framed position on the wall.

AlphaWorld and its kin—such as WorldsAway, Moondo from Intel, and PointWorld from Black Sun and and Point Communications—represent not just the next stage of the MUD, or multiuser dungeon. They represent the jump from the old technology of the imagination, *text,* to the new technology of the imagination, *virtual reality.* This is truly "ground zero" of something new: the birth of global cyberspace. The baseline goals of immersive virtual reality have been met, which is to present the virtual world as a three-dimensional space inhabited by the viewer. It is a primitive sort of virtual reality that is currently being offered, to be sure. By the standards of military simulators, or even virtual reality game machines, this stuff is crude, it is buggy, and it is balky. But it is on the Net, and you can go there now.

The goal of cyberspace is to create a medium where it is not just the message, but the messengers themselves, who are transported. As Paul Saffo of the Institute of the Future in Palo Alto put it, "the essence of cyberspace is that communication is no longer just a conduit we pass through, but a destination in its own right."[5] Or, as the creators of AlphaWorld boast, "Cyberspace is now a place."

This is the purpose of the avatar—*to take you there.* Your avatar shares a set of defining constructs—rules, laws, constraints, abilities—with the other avatar-actors. You are pioneers in the new "new world." Eventually, these images come to represent for you the people behind the digital masks—you begin to know their habits and hangouts, their likes and dislikes; you know the ones you can trust and the ones to avoid, who is an old hand and who is a newbie. And someday, in the not-too-distant future, you will have to decide who is a person and who is a machine.[6] While all this is going on, you yourself are "embodying the avatar"—you are becoming the symbol. This is the point, after all, of the design: to create an inhabitable world that supports the "full richness of human interaction."

Fluid Identities

A virtual place populated by real people, AlphaWorld takes social computing to the next level. By immigrating to AlphaWorld you become one of its citizens and help to shape it. . . . This is not some preprogrammed simulation—it is as unpredictable and unique as the individuals who help create it. Including you.[7] (From the AlphaWorld Home Page)

To Jaron Lanier (who first coined the term "virtual reality") and other cyberspace seers, the final destination of cyberspace is a world without limits, a place of infinite creative possibilities. Gone are the constraints of material bodies, of the material world, even of language. The idealized virtual reality of the future is a seamless interface between our deepest, most inexpressible wishes and desires, and the effectors in the virtual world. "Your wish is my command" becomes the operative experience of all mankind (all of "wired" mankind anyway), as the genie of magic technology does our every bidding.

The fulfillment of every technological dream begins with a single step. Interestingly, that first step in AlphaWorld is the creation of fluid identities. The avatar can be whatever one wants it to be—man, woman, child, butterfly, penguin, whatever. Even going back to the LucasFilm Habitat, whatever other capabilities may have been lacking, each avatar had at his disposal a command to change sex—from male to female or vice versa—at will. It is an important aspect of these virtual worlds, seemingly, that sexual identity (and all other forms of identity) are up for grabs. Beyond the control of personal identity, virtual world designers are now also beginning to offer inhabitants the ability to shape their surroundings.

Building Worlds

In AlphaWorld, for example, avatars are given a taste of the plastic world of the future by being able to build their own "houses." Each avatar can stake out a plot in the AlphaWorld terrain and choose from an assortment of prefabricated building materials to build the virtual dwelling of their dreams. Hurry, all the best lots are getting snatched up even as you read this!

This dream of the ideal world of the future is fueled by the notion that the imagination is the magic wand that will save us from our circumstances, the force that will free us from the decaying forms of the past, and from the constraints of sorry material existence. It is an idea that is spoon-fed to anyone who comes into contact with the pervasive organs of the mass media, which increasingly means the whole world. It seems that everyone from John Lennon to Barney (the purple dinosaur) has one message for us: "Just imagine." And this, ultimately, is the carrot of cyberspace—the place where everything will be just what we have always imagined.

In the plans for global cyberspace, there are more than faint echoes of another grand project from man's past:

> And they said, "Come, let us build ourselves a city, and a tower whose top is in the heavens; let us make a name for ourselves, lest we be scattered abroad over the face of the whole earth." And the Lord said, "Indeed the people are one and they all have one language, and this is what they begin to do; now nothing that they propose to do will be withheld from them" (Genesis 11:4-6 NKJV).

The purpose of that building project on the plains of Shinar was to create a unifying achievement that would somehow elevate man to the heavens, the level of "the gods." God, looking down upon this effort, observed that if this were to happen, "nothing they propose to do will be withheld from them." Nothing that came into the imagination of man would be impossible to achieve. This was not an outcome God was willing to allow. The tower was also a kind of idolatry of self and of what man could become; its intended result was to be security, cohesion, and uniformity. How ironic, then, that its actual result was babel.

As Santayana observed, "Those who ignore the past are destined to repeat its mistakes." Perhaps, then, it would be worthwhile, in this look at what is to come, to pause for a second to reflect on that which has already taken place.

Gods of Silicon

"Then the people bowed and prayed
To the neon god they made . . ."
— Simon & Garfunkle
"The Sound of Silence"

The subject of idolatry seems foreign to the modern mind. After all, we do not sacrifice to bronze statues, or consult the kitchen god in this day and age, do we? Nevertheless, one cannot help but be struck by the number of times believers are admonished in the pages of the Old and New Testaments to guard themselves against idolatry. The first of the Ten Commandments is this: "You shall have no other gods before me" (Exodus 20:3). *Every* writer of the New Testament warns against idolatry. Have we, then, somehow become immune to this ancient defilement?

Webster's Dictionary defines worship as "reverence offered a divine being or supernatural power; extravagant respect or admiration for or adoration to an object of esteem." Worship involves our priorities—that to which we ascribe the highest importance, or worth. That is why, for example, greed is a form of idolatry; it involves replacing God with something else, money.

Interestingly, the proscription against having "other gods" is directly tied to the prohibition against the creation of images. In Exodus 20:4, the commandment continues: "You shall not make for yourself an idol, or any likeness of what is in heaven above or on the earth beneath or in the water under the earth."

Avatars and Images

I am back in AlphaWorld. The "parachuting in" process is more or less complete. The avatar is responding to my mouse movements as I turn to survey the landscape in all directions. A little ways off, I see what appears to be a virtual newspaper stand, no doubt stocked with copies of the *AlphaWorld Times,* and I move in that direction. Maybe I will try to read one. Suddenly, my display is frozen. I try to move, but the avatar has stopped responding to the mouse. The scene in front of me is fixed. And then, after a few seconds, the screen goes blank. Suddenly I am looking at that most elemental of PC icons: "C:\" and a blinking cursor, white characters on a black background. I am out of AlphaWorld, out of Windows, and all the way back out to DOS. Strangely, I am comforted. I have gone from the cutting edge to the nothing edge in less than a minute; my 486 computer with 8 megabytes of RAM is clearly overmatched by the challenge of AlphaWorld's real-time 3-D rendering. As I sit looking at the useless screen, it occurs to me that if I cannot get into AlphaWorld, then neither can a lot of other folks. There is still a little time . . .

I have been on the plane where the superhuman abilities of the computer combine with the creative power of the human mind. It is the place where man can *be* what he wants to be, *where* he wants to be, *when* he wants to be. Rising out of this possibilities-milieu is—*the avatar,* the person we always imagined we could be. Worship of the avatar allows man to make an idol of both himself and his creation in one fell swoop. Here, then, we catch a glimpse of the new god, the god that will finally displace that angry, patriarchal god of the ancestor's imagination, the god that will finally lead us into the promised land of techno-security and multicultural uniformity.

Cyberspace is a world of images. There is nothing in cyberspace that has not been borrowed or captured from the real world of sights and sounds. The world around us is a world of living things; a place where the sea roars, the rivers clap their hands, the mountains sing together for joy before the Lord (Psalm 98). Cyberspace, on the other hand, is a world of lifeless images created by an apprentice who has not been given the secret of life. There, nothing speaks the Creator's praise; only a faint, sad echo, a paean to the dabblers, the created creators.

8

VIRTUALITY AND THEOPHOBIA

Brooks Alexander

OVERVIEW

In man's constant quest for a place to hide—all to escape an infinite God whom he cannot control or manipulate—he has perhaps found a supreme haven in his most recent creation, cyberspace. Brooks Alexander explores how this digital garden of delights promises to offer what other sanctuaries down through the centuries—from shamanism to neognosticism—could offer only in part. Now man can temporarily remake the very outward reality with which he has been at enmity since time immemorial. In cyberspace the human creator can form the laws of his own domain. He can finally become the god of his own creation.

Of course, this is true only as long as he is joined to the machines of his own creation, machines which themselves are mutable. When they fail, he is faced once again with the age-old dilemma of a universe and a God that he did not fashion. And that is the terrible conundrum of cyberspace, a digital reality that can be turned off with the mere flip of a switch. Not so with the other reality—the one that was fashioned ex nihilo *and conceived long before the world was made.*

hristianity has been called "a form of sanctified cynicism." Biblical faith means we cannot be skeptics about the supernatural, but we must be cynics about human nature.

Most people are not accustomed to thinking of cynicism as a quality of Christian thought. But the Gospel—like Christ Himself—is utterly without illusion in assessing human motive and behavior. Christianity is thoroughly cynical in recognizing human fallenness and everything it entails. It understands fully that fallen human beings are relentlessly self-seeking and grotesquely shortsighted about it; that they are born buck-passers, quick to blame and slow to accept responsibility. It understands that they obsessively seek to manipulate others (and reality in general) to their own advantage, regardless of the consequences. Most of all, it understands that fallen humans instinctively recoil from God's presence and reflexively reject His purposes—all the while concealing their real agenda from themselves and others by invoking high-minded excuses for their behavior (see Appendix C: The Other Half).

Theophobia: Hiding from God

Christian cynicism particularly knows that fallen human beings shrink from the presence of God. That evasive impulse

was the first of the new characteristics Adam and Eve exhib-
ited after their fall (Genesis 3:8). First the couple draped
themselves with the foliage of the forest. Then they tried to
disappear into the forest itself. They literally tried to hide
from God by blending in with the rest of nature: "Nobody
here but us plants and animals!"

Their offspring have continued to do the same thing,
from the beginning of history down to the present day. Our
strategies of concealment are more complex than those of
Adam and Eve, but we still hide from God for the same simple
reason they did—namely, because we are all out of harmony
with Him.

Being at odds with God means that we find ourselves in
conflict with a power we cannot even resist, much less overcome. Our so-called "contest" with God is a gross mismatch. It
is like the "contest" between a thatched hut and the force of a
hydrogen bomb.

Because of that imbalance, when we encounter the living
God, we feel not only confronted but overpowered. To put it
clinically, we feel "spiritual discomfort" of an urgent and
threatening intensity. We recoil from God's presence by spiritual reflex, just as we recoil reflexively from physical pain. It is
a visceral reaction that bypasses the thinking mind. We react
to the presence of God like an amoeba reacts to an acid solution—we freeze in shock, shrink in pain, and flee in fear and
trembling.

One of the things we do in our spiritual flight is to seek
spiritual "cover"—that is, to preemptively engage the part of
us that God wants to be connected with. We tune God out
most effectively by making sure that the spiritual part of our
nature is fully occupied with something else. Thus, we hide
from God in substitute spiritual relations—with spirits,
totems, gremlins, gods, ghosts, *devas*, demons, angels, ancestors, fairies, leprechauns, UFOs, or whatever. The void created by our estrangement from God does not stay empty for
long. As G. K. Chesterton famously remarked, "When a man

ceases to believe in God, he doesn't believe in nothing, he believes in anything."

Technology and Tech-Gnosis

Today our compulsion to flee from God is sending us into strange new hiding places that technology is opening up. Now we go looking for our preemptive spiritual connections in the labyrinths of our own computer networks. Contemporary theophobes are too sophisticated to believe in the biblical God, of course, but not too sophisticated to believe in a kind of cyber-supernaturalism that includes almost everything else. They are even ready to believe in ghosts—or at least in an up-to-date version of the "ghost in the machine." Some cyber-enthusiasts speak of the Internet as a "global mind"—created and operated by human beings, but animated by a higher, collective consciousness. Others claim that virtual reality opens a "portal to transcendence," creating a new, nonspatial world of infinite freedom that exists in and through our interactions in cyberspace—a kind of "collective hallucination" given "virtual flesh" in the patterns of digital bits and bytes that pulse through the World Wide Web.

In this way, we ourselves become the elusive presence that haunts the recesses of our own hardware and software creations. We become the animating "soul" of the works of our own hands. The prophet Isaiah derided the primitive idolator for making an object of wood or metal by his own effort and then expecting the thing to be inhabited by a "god." Today we have pressed the envelope of idolatry far beyond that primitive presumption by building artifacts for *our* divine inhabitation. *We* become the god who lives in our new techno-totem—*we are the ghost in our own machine.*

Such rarefied levels of idolatry require a hubris that has more in common with Gnosticism and self-deification than it does with idol worship in the normal sense of the term. Self-deification is the ultimate hiding place from God, and ancient

Gnosticism turned the pursuit of "the god within" into a spiritual system.

In the almost two thousand years since Gnosticism's first advent, its so-called "gnosis" has proved to be a highly effective means of hiding from God. Presently, resurgent (neo) Gnosticism is having a field day in popular culture.[1] One reason for the appeal of Gnosticism today is that our inborn tendency to gnostic thinking has been reinforced by our technology. Modern techno-culture is itself a form of "instrumental Gnosticism"—a kind of delusionary "knowledge" about reality that is mediated to us through the instruments of mass communication.

The spiritual world and the techno-world intersect in the media. Today's mass media encourage our gnostic tendencies by making the world of shared imagination seem real to begin with. Aberrant spiritual ideas flourish readily in that realm of collective fantasy. As the media reduce all events to info-tainment, the line between interpreting reality and inventing it starts to blur in the popular mind.

The cyber-revolution gives us new tools with which to take that confusion to even higher levels. Finally, we start to blur the boundaries between the personal self and ultimate reality. Gnosticism merges with technology to become tech-gnosis— that is, technologically mediated enlightenment. In cyberspace, our flight from God acquires new wings.

Gnosticism—Ancient and Modern

Original Gnosticism turned theophobia into a religion. Gnosticism created an elaborate system of distancing us from God by means of an angelic hierarchy. According to the most developed forms of gnostic theology, "God" is too pure, too spiritual, too high and holy to have any hands-on contact with the crude material world. He (or rather *It*) did not create physical reality, a lesser, flawed deity did. The pure, noncreating God is therefore separated from the impurity of the physical world by an array of angel-like beings, called *aeons*, arranged in a descending order—away from pure God, and toward gross matter.

Gnosticism offered its believers a "salvation" that committed them to a lengthy, difficult, and dangerous climb up the angelic ladder toward the goal of union with their "God." At the end of that climb lay the promise of enlightenment— the "knowledge" (*gnosis*) that gave Gnosticism its name.

Now, as then, the gnostic's all-consuming quest for enlightenment becomes a form of spiritual flight in itself. But the *purpose* of flight is safety and refuge (that is, an *end* to flight), and the state of mind called "gnosis" is therefore a final, defensive lock and seal against God. Like other forms of enlightenment, "gnosis" is a way of folding human subjectivity in upon itself, so that the unregenerate mind reflects its nature back to itself in an infinite feedback loop. It is almost impossible to penetrate that self-contained spiritual world. The false infinity of self-reflecting solipsism is a perfect refuge from the impending presence of God.

Today, neo-Gnosticism is setting up that same delusionary house of mirrors. The process of construction, however, has been streamlined, thanks to computer technology. Original Gnosticism required dedication and hard work to condition the mind for enlightenment. But computers promise to make that kind of mental discipline obsolete. Some scientists believe that with the aid of computers and neurophysiology, enlightenment can be produced without any effort—or even any intent—on the part of the enlightenee.

David Porush is a professor at Renssalear Polytechnic Institute, where he conducts research on artificial intelligence (AI). Porush envisions cyberspace as a kind of electronic designer drug:

> Neurophysiologists suspect that lurking somewhere in the brain—most likely in a formation at the base of the brain stem called the dorsal raphe nucleus—lies a facility that makes us feel, under the right conditions, like we're in communication with gods or that we have voyaged out to meet

some Higher Presence. Certain configurations of data delivered to the brain by electronic stimulation could flood this region of the brain with serotonin, a neurotransmitter involved in many functions, including hallucination. In this way, the right software might evoke that oceanic, world-embracing feeling known so well to mystics and psychotropical beachcombers.[2]

Porush's final pronouncement is not exactly what you would call a modest proposal. Cyberspace, he says, "could be our civilization's burning bush."

Occult Traffic on the Info-Bahn

Even Porush's ambitious approach to cyberspace seems mundane to many pagans and occultists. One of the real surprises of the 1980s was the emergence of a strong relationship between the magical worldview and the cybernetic mentality. The connection came to light in 1985 with the publication of *Drawing Down the Moon,* by Margot Adler (National Public Radio commentator, daughter of philosopher Mortimer Adler, and a self-identified witch). Adler's groundbreaking book was a survey of the social and spiritual history of neopaganism and modern witchcraft, with particular emphasis on current developments in North America. As part of her research, she surveyed the pagan community and discovered that

> an "amazingly high" percentage of folks drew their paychecks from technical fields and from the computer industry. Respondents gave many reasons for this curious affinity—everything from "computers are elementals in disguise" to the simple fact that the computer industry provided jobs for the kind of smart, iconoclastic and experimental folk that paganism attracts. . . . But if you dig deep enough, you find more intimate correspondences between computer culture and paganism's religion of the imagination.[3]

Such connections may seem odd to the secular mind. However, they come as no surprise to anyone who understands what a biblical worldview means. The Bible depicts occultism in general and self-deifying occultism in particular as the ultimate rejection of God (see Genesis 3:5, Isaiah 47, and Revelation 17:1-5). Biblically speaking, occultism is the last refuge of the theophobe; magic, sorcery, and spirit contact are a last barricade thrown up against the sensed approach of the presence of God. Occultism always manifests itself as a terminal form of self-will, culturally as well as personally.

As we have already noted, computer technology does the same thing all technology does—that is, it amplifies human will and purpose. It does so, however, at a staggering rate, and with universal application. Whereas earlier machines only amplified our power for *specific* purposes (for example, steam locomotives gave us power to haul loads on rails), the cyber-machine amplifies our power for literally *anything* we want to do—from manipulating genes to visualizing weather systems. And it takes weeks, not years, for the impact of its improvements to be felt.

Computers therefore empower every aspect of human nature without exception, and they do so with breathtaking speed and breadth of effect. Given what we know about human nature, that is a sobering prospect. Because theophobia has become a built-in part of human nature since the fall, we can unerringly predict that the computer revolution will greatly increase the number and power of available ways to flee from the presence of God—with particular emphasis on the more radical ways, such as techno-magic and digital spiritism.

Weaving Pagan Webs in Cyberspace

It is redundant to even speak of "prediction" at this stage—simple observation makes the point. On a sociological level alone, the neopagan movement is highly networked in cyberspace, as pagans communicate with one another through a number of occult-oriented chat rooms on the Internet. One author speaks pointedly of the Internet as "the clearinghouse of contemporary heresy."[4] Much of the neo-pagan movement's growth and a lot of its evolving practices are generated through interaction on the Net.

Cyber-savvy pagans also incorporate both computer hardware and software directly into their magical operations. Individual variations on that theme are as numerous as the individuals involved. But two examples will serve to illustrate how computers are being used as tools of magic in the quest for occult power and enlightenment.

The first example involves Tyagi (an adopted name), a 33-year-old Californian from San Jose who calls himself a practitioner of "chaos magic."

> After reading and deeply researching philosophy, mysticism and the occult, Tyagi began cobbling together his own mythic structures, divination systems and rituals—an eclectic spirituality well suited to the Net's culture of complex interconnections....."Using popular media is an important aspect of chaos magic," Tyagi says . . . "Most pagans would get online and say, 'Let's get together somewhere and do a ritual.' Chaos magicians would say, 'Let's do the ritual online.' "[5]

Tyagi is a solitary chip-monk in a silicon monastery. He spends four to six hours daily on the Internet, weaving his cyber-spells and occult Web connections. "Being online is part of my practice. It's kind of a hermit-like existence, like going into a cave. I'm not really connected to people, I'm just sending out messages and receiving them back."[6]

Computers as Magical Implements

Mark Pesce of San Francisco is a different breed of techno-pagan. He is nothing if not "connected"—being part of the gay scene, the pagan scene, and the computer scene all at once. Pesce is an ex-Catholic, ex-Pentecostal, M.I.T. dropout who is currently an author, software creator, homosexual, and witch. Pesce claims that the Craft is "nothing less than applied cybernetics." Computers and computer programs can be magical objects or even sacred objects, he says, because they "embody our communication with each other *and with the entities—the divine parts of ourselves—that we invoke in that space.*"[7]

Pesce uses physical computers to help frame the metaphysical space that ceremonial magic seeks to create. For example, he recently celebrated a "Cyber-Samhain"—his own

> digitally enhanced version of the ancient Celtic celebration of the dead known to the rest of us as Halloween. Of all of paganism's seasonal festivals, Samhain (pronounced "saw-when") is the ripest time for magic. As most pagans will tell you, it's the time when the veils between the worlds of the living and the dead are thinnest. For Pesce, Samhain is a perfect time to ritually bless *Worldview* [his new computer program] as a passageway between the meat world and the electronic shadow land of the Net.[8]

Pesce's cyber-ceremony is typically neopagan in that it follows the traditional occult practice of "casting a circle," within which the ritual is to be performed and the magic is to occur. In most traditions of ceremonial magic, the circle is seen as a zone of protection from the dangerous forces the magician is calling forth. But neopagans see the circle as a way of creating a special place with room for spirits to be and magic to happen—a metaphysical enclave set up in the midst of a mundane world that has no room for metaphysics.

Pesce's ritual updates the casting of the magical circle by using computers to mark both its physical and metaphysical boundaries.

> Pagans carve out tightly bounded zones in both physical and psychic space . . . the stage is often set by invoking the four elements that the ancients believed composed all

matter. Often symbolized by colored candles or statues, these four "Watchtowers" stand like imaginary sentinels in the four cardinal directions of the circle.

But tonight's Watchtowers are four PCs networked through an ethernet and linked to a SPARCstation with an Internet connection . . . The four monitors face into the circle, glowing patiently in the subdued light. Each machine is running *Worldview,* and each screen shows a different angle on a virtual space . . . a ritual circle that mirrors the one Pesce will create in the room. . . .

A roomful of geeks, techno-yuppies and multimedia converts circle around in the monitor glow, chanting and laughing. . . . I join in with pleasure. . . . We are woven into a world without which we are nothing, and our glittering electronic nets are not separate from that ancient webwork.[9]

The End of Theophobia

Magic and technology are two versions of the same impulse—*the impulse to self-will*—and it is inevitable that they reconverge. It is no accident that our feats of computer technology are rising to the level of virtual magic at the same time that we are embracing computers as instruments of actual magic.

The result of that partnership will be a new and improved refuge from God, a uniquely enthralling and widespread delusion not seen before in the history of the world. Computers have empowered our God-avoidance reflex along with everything else. In cyberspace we are constructing not just a spiritual hiding place, but a spiritual bomb-shelter. In the end, of course, our shelter will prove completely useless. In His own timing, God blows through our most well-prepared defenses as though they are not even there.

In the meantime, however, we should expect the theophobic delusions that flourish in cyberspace to intensify. They will also become increasingly influential socially and politically—at least within the context of collective consent that sustains them. Those who do not consent to the delusion will be marginalized at best, since computers will increasingly dominate human life, and tech-gnostic delusion will increasingly dominate the computer elite.

No matter how strong the power of collective consent may be in human terms, however, in God's terms it remains a closed circle of denial and self-deceit. Its *reality* remains *virtual*—and therefore impotent in the face of *actual* reality. We should not forget that through His sovereignty over nature, God has some serious options available for upsetting our theophobic schemes. We may be the ghost in our own machine, but our machine is more fragile than we imagine. What happens to the "collective hallucination" when the power-grid goes down? Does its "virtual flesh" moulder in a virtual grave, awaiting virtual resurrection?

Science fiction writer Philip K. Dick said, "reality is that which doesn't go away when you stop believing in it." Today we could add ". . . or cut off the electricity." In the face of God's actual reality, theophobia—even computer-enhanced, virtually realized theophobia—has all the prospects of the proverbial snowball in hell. The fallen delusions that haunt cyberspace may be impenetrable to us, but they are utterly transparent to God.

A Final Word

LOST IN THE GARDEN OF DIGITAL DELIGHTS

Tal Brooke

The present dawn of cyberspace is still barely a land of shadow figures compared to what it will become when the current technology is fully powered up. The combination of factors needed for this to happen is obvious—faster, sleeker technology with leaps in memory capacity, transmission speed, and central processor power. Computers alone have increased in power more than 100,000-fold in the past 50 years, and the other components of cyberspace will not remain far behind.

When the present trickle of data that animates cyberspace with crude motion and sound effects at 28,800-baud jumps up to millions of baud (which is already starting to happen in some instances, as in Pacific Bell's Asymmetric Digital Subscriber Line)—when the interactive gear becomes affordable and downsized—when virtual reality enters in full-bodied form, *then* some of our projections in this book will become realities. A very powerful beast will be standing in the town square of history probably at the start of the next millennium.

Commerce is positioned to explode over this new medium according to international business consultant, Harvard professor, and best-selling author Peter F. Drucker.

Throughout his latest book, *Managing in a Time of Great Change*, Drucker boldly asserts that cyberspace will be the new conduit for global commerce, revolutionizing international business and finance in a way that comes only every other century. Meanwhile, governments and their agencies, the military, universities, media conglomerates, communications giants, and practically every other major entity is preparing for this quantum shift. Books by the score will be coming out that explore the practical domains of cyberspace.

Our interest in this book has been in the human interface of a technology that seems destined to reach every population and age-group in the world—one that has serious spiritual and moral dimensions. From the spiritual summit, our interest is even more finely tuned, for we see a new theater of operations for what has been an ageless war over the human soul.

Technology in and of itself is a neutral medium available for good or evil purposes. The most primitive tool such as the axe can be used for killing (a preferred weapon in medieval times) or for cutting down trees. Sophisticated instruments such as the television can equally be used for good or evil, but with a broader spectrum of gradations. As the forerunner of cyberspace, the television offers us an index of how cyberspace will be used. Out of 100 cable channels, five might be truly "good," constructive, and educational; 25 are less so; and the remaining channels contain shows that not only *are not* edifying, they seduce audiences and constantly push the envelope by broadening the terrain of incest, homosexuality, and the like. This trend has been obvious for years. If the range in public taste in cable TV is any indication, cyberspace will take the same course, and that is not good.

In reality, the entire bell-shaped curve of television programming has been incrementally shifting to the left for 40 years. Howard Sterne on the Entertainment network, Beavis and Butthead on MTV, among many others, could not have existed in the 1950s. The atmosphere of our culture could not have absorbed such programming then. This is obviously true with dedicated adult channels such as Penthouse that specialize in porn and violence. The advent of such entertainment has produced a certain moral tenderizing of the masses over decades. How far this slide continues, and what happens when it switches to the much more powerful instrument of cyberspace (where these experiences can be explored *interactively*), remains a key concern.

The Digital Game Room

For countless young cyber-enthusiasts, the fully powered technology of cyberspace will bring today's most sophisticated role-playing and arcade games right into their homes. Except these games will be much more engaging than anything that exists today. Even virtual reality games that cost eight dollars a pop at such progressive venues as club DV8 in San Francisco will seem grainy and cartoonlike compared to what is up ahead.

It will be a temptation for any youth to spend time in this realm, especially the growing hoard of disaffected youth from families that are barely limping through life. They will have every reason to escape into cyberspace. Each home will have an escape hatch, but it will not be the comparatively benign attic portal into the land of Narnia that we read about in C. S. Lewis's "Chronicles of Narnia."

Twenty years ago when kids wanted to steal off for a private meeting, they often resorted to playing hooky from school or climbing out the upstairs window at night. But soon they can just lock their rooms, put on a helmet with panoramic viewing, log in, enter the digital plane, pick the designer body fitting their mood, grab some digital surfboards, and go blazing down some three-dimensional tunnel while laughing and joking with their friends. They will also have easy access to new realms of experience beyond their years in this garden of digital delights.

It will be the same thing for adults who learn they can so easily meet on the sly—the old story of the bored husband or wife who wants a quick and safe fling without any dirty footprints leading back to the bedroom. Of course, it may lead to the real thing very quickly. But the anonymous meeting in a cyber-room will always remain an inviting temptation for illicit liaisons. No bars or hotel rooms; just a tete-a-tete somewhere in cyberspace. But that is only the starting point for the infinitely variegated human imagination. The garden of digital delights will offer many more diversions. Some, of course, will be unspeakably dark.

A unique problem could surface when it comes time for the cyber-generation to take off its gear and face the workaday world with its responsibilities and drudgery. Some users will never want to log off. Others will prefer their own domain of alternate worlds above the rough ride of life, especially teens who face the inevitable trials unique to adolescence—trials that are so necessary for healthy character formation.

Cyber-dependency is inevitable. We have already seen what constant indulgence in television and drugs has done to stunt succeeding generations of youth who have emerged—each a little slower, duller, less motivated, and less equipped to resist life's pressures than preceding waves. Cyberspace will offer more kicks. So far we have seen that those who become really hooked—with drugs and alcohol at the moment—readily collapse in the face of temptation only to seek further escape, fueling their inability to deal with the demands of life in the real world. A cyber-dependent generation could become what George Orwell, Aldous Huxley, and Aleksandr Isayevich Solzhenitsyn have each described in varying ways—weakened characters controlled by pleasure and pain who can so easily become putty in the hands of the all-powerful State. Put another way, what better way of domesticating a generation is there than loosing it in the garden of digital delights where it will lose the will to resist and the inner character to fight.

The dangers of cyberspace are very real. After its unique and "beneficial" offerings of unlimited information, mind expansion, full-body interaction, instant commerce, long-distance medical diagnosis, global home offices, and a whole cornucopia of other services, older deeper hungers could awaken. So could an increasing dependency arise on the mechanical genie itself in virtually every area of life. The final Devil's bargain would become evident: Seeking the illusion of unlimited freedom, people will become hooked to a machine that will hold them in a tighter grip than any prison before it, capturing the very soul.

The beast that is able to enter the human mind like an open door can also invade history with a strength unrivaled in the past—appearing first as a servant, then becoming a terrible weapon over a people, over a population.

Man's Perennial Dilemma

Ever since the terrible event in Eden, when man chose the false promise of godhood and immortality over the *Viseo Dei*— the ineffable splendor of God's presence—he has been allowed to suffer the folly of his choice. In a mere instant what had been an innocent and pellucid consciousness was flooded with an expanding darkness that stained the conscience and forever changed the human soul. Innocence and purity fled like the vanishing light of dusk.

With the sudden knowledge of evil came loneliness and alienation. Down the dark centuries that followed, depravities of all varieties cascaded from human experience: wars, murder, and all manner of cruelty—"man's inhumanity to man"— spread through history. The self-will of human nature was in a constant hunt for acquisition, pleasure, and conquest, despite the outcome. A troubled conscience became man's constant companion, forever haunted by the evils it had done and would continue to do.

To escape this troubled conscience, man has tried again and again to find sanctuary, to remake reality by blotting God out of his awareness. One such sanctuary has been those religions and beliefs that assuaged his conscience and assured him that there is no holy God to judge his life; that there are no real and permanent consequences for evil; and that his true inner nature is divinity itself. Those beliefs reached full development in ancient Babylon and India. The same beliefs have now come back as the New Age movement. The synchronicity of such beliefs arriving with the birth of cyberspace promises to fulfill man's desperate quest for an alternative reality, a place to hide.

A place to hide. The final seamless sanctuary from reality is indeed something that cyberspace—the beast that now stands in the town square of history—could offer in bounty, this garden of digital delights. The imagination can run free in the planes of cyberspace where digital reality is plastic and can be altered and reinvented at whim. The self can be endlessly redefined. It can appear as its own electronic "avatar" and descend godlike into worlds that it invents—until it runs into its own trap and becomes enslaved. The consequence is to be endlessly frozen within a universe of one's own making by playing God. Suddenly the patient has entered the darkest ward of the madhouse only to lock himself permanently in the inner chamber.

Delusion is the consequence of fleeing reality. It is the outcome of rejecting God and all He has created. It is the worst kind of alienation—from reality and from God. Should such delusion finally descend upon the world, as the apostle John indicates in the book of Revelation, then time will come full circle and the folly of Eden will have reaped its terrible harvest at the end of history.

The only remedy to a world lost in delusion will be when the eschaton arrives and God intervenes. The Son of Man, as is recorded, will appear with an effulgence that tears apart the fabric of any manmade pretense in a thunderous awaking for the world. Not even the most powerful delusion will be able to withstand the light of His coming. Nor can it spare the multitudes from seeing the reality of what they have become. The full magnitude of choice will be revealed and no one will be able to turn away from this reckoning—both an end and a new beginning.

Appendix A

TECHNOLOGY AND THE FALL

The fall did not create technology, but it set the direction for our pursuit of it. The fall determines our reasons for inventing technology, it determines how we use technology, and it determines the results that will flow from that use. Indeed, it is not overstating the case to say that the serpent's temptation to Adam and Eve implicitly promised a certain kind of "godlike" technological prowess.

Remember that the serpent first slandered God by insinuating that He is a selfish and mean-spirited deceiver. He then made three baited promises to Eve from his repertoire of deception:

> And the serpent said unto the woman, "Ye shall not surely die! For God doth know that in the day ye eat thereof, then your eyes shall be opened, and ye shall be as gods, knowing good and evil" (Genesis 3:4-5 KJV).

The opening of the eyes to good and evil is basic to the promise of godlikeness. It is not clear in the English translation, but in the original Hebrew the concept of good and evil carries a clear implication of technological power. In the Hebrew mind-set, good and evil are more than just moral categories. The words also signify "useful" and "useless." Echoes of that meaning still exist in English today. We say that a hammer is "good" (that is, "useful") for driving nails, but it is "not good" (that is, "useless") for turning screws.

The ability to make that distinction is the foundation of all technology. And the useful and useless are only distinguishable on the basis of some purpose that one has in mind. In an unfallen world our primal parents might have graduated to an anointed form of technology that served the purposes of God for our self-expression and our growth in harmony with Him and His creation. But that is not the world we live in. In the real world, the fall has distorted the development of our technology by distorting the purposes that define how we think about the issue of useful versus useless to begin with.

How do we arrive at the purposes that define our technologies? The fall involves, above everything else, the turning away from God and toward self for all our reference points. Now our own self-perceived requirements dominate our attention. Cut loose from God's purposes, we devise our own purposes, and those purposes determine what we consider "useful" and what we discard as "useless."

Technology and Hiding

How did the fruits of that new technological power first appear to Adam and Eve? The first new purpose they acquired was that of seeking concealment, and the first thing they did was to stitch some concealment together.

> And the eyes of them both were opened, and they knew that they were naked; and they sewed fig leaves together, and made themselves aprons (Genesis 3:7 KJV).

Recall what the serpent had promised. He had said that their eyes would be opened, and they would know good and evil. Here we are told that their eyes *were* in fact opened. And what did they know? They knew they were naked—and they knew what to do about it.

It is significant that this is the first form taken by their new "godlike" knowledge. They could only know their "nakedness" in relation to a standard of self-concern. But Adam and Eve did not acquire their new self-standard in one stroke.

When Eve took the fruit in order to be "wise," she was already looking for self-initiated change apart from any reference to God. Eve had gone that far in her own heart before eating anything. In the act of eating, her desire turned into behavior. And behavior produced its results. In their knowledge of nakedness, Adam and Eve's newly acquired "knowledge of good and evil" came to its pragmatic conclusion.

Through the fall, the world becomes alien and threatening, and we react to that fact with self-centered anxiety. Adam and Eve's perception of their own nakedness is based on a standard of self-need, and their response is an act of self-help—the first recorded act of technology, if you will. This is the pivotal point at which the "knowledge of good and evil" comes into play—including the knowledge of the "useful" and the "useless"—and it turns out to be something of a letdown. Adam and Eve have indeed become "like God"—just not *very much* like Him.

The fig leaves were essentially an effort to "conceal" the responsible selves. The fig leaves had less to do with concealing the sexual parts than most people think. More fundamentally, they had to do with concealing guilt by blending the human identity into the background pattern of nature as a whole. After draping themselves with the products of nature, Adam and Eve further hid themselves from the presence of God "among the trees of the garden" ("Nobody here but us plants and animals!").

That basic evasive impulse to hide by blending into the background accounts for a great deal of mysticism, especially "nature mysticism." As the natural self dissolves back into nature, so does the spiritual burden it bears. To a self under the judgment of God, self-dissolution seems like a reprieve. Thus the appeal of Buddhistic enlightenment: the world dissolves into process—and the self is part of that dissolving world. *There is no one to be judged if there is no one at all!*

Such dedicated self-concealment is a form of self-confession and, paradoxically, a form of self-retribution. Denis de Rougemont speaks of the dilemma of guilt and denial, as the conscience faces an overwhelming reality it can neither acknowledge nor avoid.

> Here we find set into motion the complicated mechanisms of the perversion, of the self-punishment of a torn conscience, and of the desire to destroy oneself at last, to destroy oneself in order to make oneself innocent!—in order still to escape the consequences of what the evil one has done; to chastise oneself without making reparations. It is the mystery of suicide and the logic of Judas; the last temptation, the supreme utopia.[1]

Of course, it does not work any better than Adam and Eve's effort to vanish into the greenery of the garden. God called them forth by name and confronted them with His presence, which they were hiding from in the first place. Once the two guilty selves were in the presence of God, the squirming commenced. When the pressure of reality began to hurt, then the sorry parade of excuses and blaming began. We have no reason to believe that our hiding will be any more successful—or that our response to being found out will be any more honorable. Even if we destroy our body with fire, ravage our personality with drugs, or dissolve our identity with mystical mental tricks, we will still be called forth by name in the resurrection. Then what?

The "Wisdom" of Self

It is clear that the "wisdom" that Adam and Eve's eyes were opened to depends on acquiring a purpose that proceeded from themselves alone. The whole concept of the knowledge of good and evil in this sense involves a decision on the part of human beings to replace God with self as the ultimate standard of reference. It involves a decision to replace God's self-disclosure with the finite needs and desires of the human self, as understood by that self. That is the fundamental turning of the will.

The immediate result of that turning is a radical contraction of consciousness. This, strictly speaking, is what is known as the "fall." Before, both Adam and Eve were resonating with the purposes of God, and were conscious of their relationship with Him. Now they are focused on themselves, drawing their awareness away from God and bringing it inward. Now everything springs from their own perception of their own needs. They have invented humanism—*and it does not work.*

It does not work any better today than it did on day one. Nor will it work any better tomorrow. Perhaps Thoreau said it best: "Our inventions are wont to be pretty toys, which distract our attention from serious things. They are but improved means to an unimproved end."

Thereby hangs the tale of human technology. It promises solutions and delivers new versions of the problem. It does so because it empowers fallen human nature, and fallen human nature is problematic to begin with.

Appendix B
ELECTRIC
COMMUNITIES

The creation of a complex virtual world such as Alpha-World represents great sums of money in development and maintenance costs. Is there really that much interest in creating on-line fantasy/adventure games and cyber-chat areas? What is behind all of this development of cyberspace anyway?

As usual, the dictum "follow the money trail" yields results. Or, in this case, the "e-money trail," because the answer appears to be that cyberspace is being made ready for global commerce. As many observers have noted, no one is making money on the Net—at least not yet. But the commercial promise of the worldwide Net is fabulous, and many entities are quietly, or not so quietly, working to make the Net safe for buying and selling in the near future. Visa International, for one, is working seriously, in conjunction with Microsoft and MasterCard, on the problem of making the Net safe for bankcards.

Visa's vision goes beyond just making the Net safe for credit card transactions as we know them. Visa wants to expand the role of the card from simply storing information about your bank account to storing *all* your personal information—driver's license, medical history, *everything*. These so-called "smart cards" figure strongly in Visa's picture of the future. To quote Daniel Akst of the *Los Angeles Times*:

Visa's plan is for these know-it-all cards to be issued by your bank. Since a microchip on the card would have plenty of room for other kinds of data, it seems inevitable that such cards would soon be indispensable, almost like a driver's license, and might similarly devolve into a de facto identity card—at least until a better technology comes along. "In 15 years, it may not be a card at all," says Carl F. Pascarella, president of Visa USA. "It could be your palm."[1]

Where else is Visa putting its money? Into AlphaWorld. Visa International is one of three major investors in San Francisco-based Worlds Inc. (creators of AlphaWorld), along with UB Networks and Pearson PLC. The creators of the original Habitat, Chip Morningstar and F. Randall Farmer of Lucas-Film, reached the conclusion, based on their observations of this early virtual world, that true commerce on the Net could only take place in a virtual world that afforded the "entire range of human interaction." This virtual world would be a place where people could meet, form opinions about one another, reasonably expect to find each other again, and so forth. In other words, they concluded that cyber-commerce could only be conducted in the context of a "habitat." It is a conclusion that has not been lost on the developers of cyberspace who have followed. This accounts for the increasing interest in avatars. This is why Visa International is sinking money into AlphaWorld, why Microsoft is sinking money into virtual chat areas on its own network, and so forth. And this is why Morningstar, Farmer, and another collaborator from the LucasFilm Habitat days, Douglas Crockford, founded an outfit called "Electric Communities."

Electric Communities is a player in the giant sweepstakes of trying to turn the Net into a global commerce vehicle, and their vision may be the most comprehensive of all those currently in the game. The goal of Electric Communities is nothing less than the establishment of the basic protocols of all global commerce, embodied in something they call the Global Cyberspace Protocols (GCP). To this end, Electric

Communities recently released a new programming language, "E," which is a superset of the popular "Java" language created by Sun Microsystems. What Hypertext Markup Language (HTML) is to the web, and what Virtual Reality Modeling Language (VRML) is to 3-D cyber-worlds, Electric Communities hopes "E" will become to global commerce applications: *the de facto standard programming language.* They plan to follow this up shortly with the release of something called the "Cyberspace Operating System" (COS), which they hope will become the DOS of the Net of the future—that is, the operating system upon which all other applications are built.

Whether they succeed remains to be seen. But one thing is certain: the avatar they helped create is coming on strong as a contender to be your personal agent in cyberspace. From the virtual chat areas of the Microsoft Network, to the strange lunar worlds of Intel's Moondo, to the vast expanses of Alpha-World and beyond, the avatars have landed—and they are waiting for you.

Appendix C

THE
OTHER HALF

In the absence of redemption, cynicism is simply despair. In the light of redemption, however, cynicism is truly the ground of hope, as the universal failings of our fallen race are met and overcome in the universal Savior.

The Gospel asserts both sides of that redemptive paradox. Christ converts the works of evil to the purposes of God, yet He still affirms the wickedness of sin. Christ does not excuse the wrongness of the evil He confronts, but neither is He content to merely punish it in retaliatory judgment. Instead, through His crucifixion, He achieves a much deeper and more far-reaching victory. In His sacrifice, Christ turns evil inside out by reversing its meaning: from bad to good, from wrong to right, from defeat to victory—and above all, from death to life. He purges wrong of its wrongness by making it serve His love: "You meant evil . . . but God meant it for good" (Genesis 50:20).

God's modus operandi reverses evil from within, as the works of evil are turned (in the end) to the service of God. God's ability to weave the artifacts of evil into the pattern of His goodness is the heart of the Good News and the meaning of the Incarnation. It is also the delightful irony of the Gospel: Christ (the innocent one) submits to His death, and to the "triumph of injustice" that it represents, and His submission gives rise to the Resurrection, which overthrows injustice as well as death. As the Russian Orthodox liturgy puts it,

"Christ has risen from the dead, trampling down death by death."

That ironic paradox of the Gospel means that "sanctified cynicism" is more than an oxymoron. It means that Christians can have a realistic, clear-eyed view of the fallen world without succumbing to the bleak despair that normally accompanies such knowledge.

About the Editors and Contributors

Brooks Alexander

Brooks Alexander is the founder of SCP (Spiritual Counterfeits Project) and currently acts as its research director. He earned a degree in political science from Texas Christian University and did five years of graduate work in international politics (at Texas Christian) and law (at the University of Texas) before he "turned on, tuned in, and dropped out" in 1963 to become part of the emerging drug and occult counterculture. He migrated to New York City, then to California, arriving in Los Angeles the day the Watts riots started. He later became part of the Haight-Ashbury scene in 1967. Alexander became a Christian in 1969 in Berkeley and founded SCP in 1973 to help Christians and others understand the changes that our culture is undergoing.

Donald L. Baker

Donald L. Baker is a telecommunications analyst and writer interested in the intersection of technology with culture and the arts. He has contributed to *World, The World & I,* and other publications. He lives near Washington, D.C., with his wife and three children, and in cyberspace at HyperReal@aol.com.

TAL BROOKE

Tal Brooke, president and chairman of SCP, Inc., is author of the bestseller *When the World Will Be As One* and four other books, including *Lord of the Air*, which chronicles his years in India as the top Western disciple of the famed "god-man" of signs and wonders Sai Baba. He has degrees from the University of Virginia and Princeton and has spoken at Oxford and Cambridge numerous times as well as other prominent universities.

JOHN MOORE

John Moore works at SCP part-time while he writes a book and helps raise two daughters. John recently participated in U.C. Berkeley's Boalt Hall Law School, one of the few doctoral students admitted into this prized and highly specialized program. Feeling called by God to other work, he left the program. His wife, Bettina, also attended Boalt Hall.

NOTES

Introduction

1. George Santayana, *The Life of Reason,* 5 vols. (New York: Dover Publications, 1905-06).

Chapter 1—Cyberspace: Storming Digital Heaven

1. Philip Elmer-Dewitt, "Welcome to Cyberspace," *Time,* Special Issue, Spring 1995.

2. Philip Elmer-Dewitt, "Cyberpunk!" *Time,* 15 October 1993.

3. Ibid.

4. George Gilder, "Scoping Out the Data Highway," interviewed by Mary Eisenhart, *Microtimes,* 25 July 1994.

5. Ibid.

6. Elmer-Dewitt, "Welcome to Cyberspace."

7. Philip Elmer-Dewitt, "Battle for the Soul of the Internet," *Time,* 25 July 1994.

8. James Fallows, "Not Yet Net," *The Atlantic Monthly,* May 1995.

9. Elmer-Dewitt, "Battle for the Soul."

10. Elmer-Dewitt, "Cyberpunk!"

11. Hannah Bloch, Wendy Cole, and Sharon E. Epperson, "Cyberporn," *Time,* 26 June 1995.

12. Prodigy Interactive News Services, 22 November 1994.

13. Elmer-Dewitt, "Battle for the Soul."

14. Jerry Carroll, "The Spoiler in Cyberspace," *The San Francisco Chronicle*, 25 April 1995.

15. Victor Keegan, "The Guardian," *London*, 12 December 1994.

16. Note: I report a different visionary/dream in the last chapter of *When the World Will Be As One*. (Harvest House Publishers felt it would inundate the reader to add this as well.)

17. Robert Wright and Mitch Kapor, "Data Highway Guru. The New Democrat from Cyberspace," *Wired*, 7 May 1993.

18. Thomas Molnar, "Oh, Benares," quoted in *SCP Newsletter*, Summer 1985, p. 22.

Chapter 2—Welcome to the Cyber-millennium

1. William J. Mitchell, *City of Bits: Space, Place, and the Infobahn* (Cambridge, MA: The M.I.T. Press, 1995), p. 167.

2. John Perry Barlow, "The Great Work," *Communications of the ACM,* January 1992. Text available at the Electronic Frontier Foundation's World Wide Web site (http://www.eff.org).

3. John Lukacs begins his book, *The End of the Twentieth Century and the End of the Modern Age* (New York: Ticknor & Fields, 1993), this way: "The twentieth century is now over. It was a short century. It lasted seventy-five years—from 1914 to 1989. Its two main events were the two world wars." He goes on to discuss in depth his concept of centuries as eras, rather than 100-year blocks.

4. This was the explicit message delivered at the G7 Information Society Conference in Brussels, February 1995, which focused on encouraging the worldwide implementation of advanced information technologies.

5. Gene Edward Veith, *Postmodern Times: A Christian Guide to Contemporary Thought and Culture* (Wheaton, IL: Crossway Books, 1994), pp. 28-29.

6. See *SCP Journal,* vol. 16:4 (1992), "Education: Capturing Hearts and Minds for a New World."

7. Michael Thompson, "Kids of the Future," *Ministries Today*, March/April 1994. Thompson's six other "sociological shapers" are: demographic polarity, the breakdown of the family, stress, moral relativism, ethnic diversity, and ecological greening.

8. John Perry Barlow, "Crime and Puzzlement," 1990. Available at the Electronic Frontier Foundation's World Wide Web site (http://www.eff.org).

9. John Perry Barlow and Mitchell Kapor, "Across the Electronic Frontier," 1990. Available at the Electronic Frontier Foundation's World Wide Web site (http://www.eff.org).

10. Page Smith, "The Expansion of New England," *American Urban History*, 2d ed., ed. Alexander B. Callow, Jr. (New York: Oxford University Press, 1973), pp. 98, 102.

11. I have liberated the forward- and backward-looking motifs from their Marxist context in: Dale Bradley, "Situating Cyberspace," Public 11: Throughput, p. 11 (Toronto: Public Access, 1995).

12. For a good history of the Internet, see chapter 3 in Howard Rheingold, *The Virtual Community: Homesteading on the Electronic Frontier* (Reading, MA: Addison Wesley Publishing Company, 1993).

13. Barlow made this remark in a 4-way, 12-page debate published as "What Are We Doing On-Line?" in the August 1995 *Harper's* magazine: "I don't say that these changes are good. I certainly don't claim we're creating a utopia. I mean, I love the physical world. I spent seventeen years as a cattle rancher in Pinedale, Wyoming. I was basically living in the nineteenth century. If I could still make a living there, I would. But the fact is, there is little economic room in the physical world these days" (p. 36).

14. S. Boxx, "Re: electracy," uploaded to Internet newsgroup alt.politics.datahighway, 16 June 1994.

15. Derrick de Kerckhove, *The Skin of Culture: Investigating the New Electronic Reality* (Toronto: Somerville House Publishing, 1995), p. 62.

16. Langdon Winner, "Mythinformation," in John Zerzan and Alice Carnes, eds., *Questioning Technology: Tool, Toy or Tyrant?* (Philadelphia: New Society Publishers, 1991), pp. 166-67.

17. Michael Novak, "Awakening from Nihilism: The Templeton Prize Address," *First Things*, August/September 1994, pp. 21-22.

18. Laurie Flynn, "The Serious Money Hits the Superhighway," *The New York Times*, 26 June 1995, p. D5.

19. Michael Sorkin, "Scenes from the Electronic City," *I.D. Magazine*, May–June 1992, pp. 73, 75.

20. David Lochhead, *Theology in a Digital World* (Canada: The United Church Publishing House, 1988), pp. 93, 94.

Chapter 3—Virtual Man

1. Mel Seesholtz, "Exotechnology: Human Efforts to Evolve Beyond Human Being," in "Thinking Robots, an Aware Internet, and Cyberpunk Librarians," a collection of background essays prepared for the 1992 LITA (Library and Information Technology Program) President's Program at the 1992 ALA annual conference.

2. Interview: Jaron Lanier, chief scientist of VPL research, *Computer Graphics World*, April 1992, vol. 15, no. 4, p. 61.

3. Alvin Toffler, *Future Shock* (New York: Random House, 1970), p. 187.

4. In fairness, it must be pointed out that Toffler also noted the potential for development in the other direction. In *Future Shock*, Toffler theorizes that robot research could ultimately lead to "the direct link-up of the human brain—stripped of its supporting physical structures—with the computer. Indeed, it may be that the biological component of the super-computers of the future may be massed human brains" (p. 189).

Toffler then goes on to cite experimental evidence from the day that the brain could be sustained, at least for limited periods, as a separate biological unit. The implications of this line of thought are truly frightening. More on this later.

5. John Perry Barlow, "Crime and Puzzlement: In Advance of the Law on the Electronic Frontier," *Whole Earth Review*, 22 September 1990, no. 68, p. 44.

6. These numbers are taken from an article, "Pre-Wired," by Michelle Vranizan in *UCLA Magazine*, Fall 1994. With the rapid growth the Internet is experiencing, it is difficult to get accurate figures on the total number of nodes and users now on the network.

7. See Hans Moravec, *Mind Children: The Future of Robot and Human Intelligence* (Cambridge: Harvard University Press, 1988), and "Letter from Moravec to Pembrose," in "Thinking Robots, an Aware Internet, and Cyberpunk Librarians."

8. "Open letter from Moravec to Penrose," 9 February 1990, posted to sci.nanotech (Internet Usenet newsgroup).

Chapter 4—The Faustian Bargain

1. An anonymous Berkeley Coffee House saga.

2. Jacques Ellul, *The Technological Bluff* (Grand Rapids: Eerdmans, 1990), p. xiv.

3. Ibid., p. 35.

4. Ibid., p. 39, emphasis in the original.

5. David Ehrenfeld, *The Arrogance of Humanism* (New York: Oxford University Press, 1978), pp. 5, 10.

6. Clifford Stoll, *Silicon Snake Oil: Second Thoughts on the Information Highway* (New York: Doubleday, 1995), pp. 95-96.

7. Ibid., pp. 60-63.

8. David Noble, "The Truth About the Information Super Highway," *Loompanics*, Spring 1995, pp. 9, 10.

9. Stoll, *Silicon Snake Oil*, p. 26.

10. Ibid., n.p.

11. Denis de Rougemont, *The Devil's Share* (New York: Meridian Books, 1944; reprint ed. 1956), p. 13.

12. Arthur Kroker and Michael Weinstein, *Data Trash: The Theory of the Virtual Class* (New York: St.Martin's Press, 1994), pp. 1-2.

13. Erik Davis, "Technosis, Magic, Memory, and the Angels of Information," *The South Atlantic Quarterly*, Fall 1993; vol. 92, no. 4, pp. 610-11.

14. Ellul, *Technological Bluff*, p. 72.

Chapter 6— Virtual Gods, Designer Universes

1. Howard Rheingold, "Douglas Trumball's Big Budget VR," *Wired*, 1.5.

2. Ibid.

3. Ibid.

4. David Kupelian, "Virtual Reality: The Drug of the Year 2000," Chancellor Broadcasting Company.

5. Burr Snider, "The Toy Story," *Wired*, 3.12.

6. W. Wayt Gibb, *Scientific American*, December 1994, vol. 271, no. 6, p. 40.

7. Ibid.

8. Eric Davis, "Technopagans," *Wired*, 3.07, July 1995.

9. Ibid.

10. Dialogue from the movie *Total Recall*.

11. Snider, "Toy Story."

Chapter 7—Virtual Bodies in the City of Bits

1. N. Katherine Hayles, "Embodied Virtuality," in Mary Anne Moser with Douglas MacLeod, eds., *Immersed in Technology: Art and Virtual Environments* (Cambridge: The MIT Press, 1996), p. 1. Hayles is a professor of English at UCLA.

2. Michael Sorkin, "Scenes from the Electronic City," *I.D. Magazine*, May–June 1992.

3. Simon Penny, "Virtual Reality as the Completion of the Enlightenment Project," in Gretchen Bender and Timothy Rucker, eds., *Culture on the Brink: Ideologies of Technology* (Seattle: Bay Press, 1994), p. 247. Penny is an associate professor of art and robotics at Carnegie Mellon University.

4. Brian J. Walsh and J. Richard Middleton, *The Transforming Vision: Shaping a Christian World View* (Downers Grove, IL: InterVarsity Press, 1984), p. 64.

5. Kenneth J. Gergen, *The Saturated Self: Dilemmas of Identity in Contemporary Life* (New York: Basic Books, 1992), p. 36.

6. Scott Bukatman, *Terminal Identity: The Virtual Subject in Postmodern Science Fiction* (Durham, NC: Duke University Press, 1993), p. 245.

7. Nell Tenhaaf, "Mysteries of the Bioapparatus," in Moser and MacLeod, *Immersed in Technology*, pp. 67-68.

8. Rob Milthorp, "Fascination, Masculinity, and Cyberspace," in Moser and MacLeod, *Immersed in Technology*, p. 137. Milthorp is an interdisciplinary artist, writer, and academic dean at the Alberta College of Art and Design in Calgary.

9. Kathy Acker, interviewed by Larry McCaffery, "Reading the Body," *Mondo 2000*, #4 (1991).

10. Gene Edward Veith, Jr., *Postmodern Times: A Christian Guide to Contemporary Thought and Culture* (Wheaton, IL: Crossway Books, 1994), p. 61. This is an excellent overview of the postmodern scene by an astute and trustworthy observer.

11. Stelarc, "Redesigning the Body—Redefining What Is Human," *Whole Earth Review*, Summer 1989, p. 18ff. Further information is available at Stelarc's World Wide Web site: (www.merlin.com.au/stelarc/).

12. Moser and MacLeod, *Immersed in Technology*, p. 2.

13. See chapter 3, "Cyborg Citizens," in William J. Mitchell, *City of Bits: Space, Place, and the Infobahn* (Cambridge: The M.I.T. Press, 1995), for an extended discussion of this likely near-future scenario.

14. Richard V. Kelly, Jr., "Abundant Worlds and Virtual Personas," *Virtual Reality* Special Report, November/December 1995, pp. 35-43.

15. My discussion of gender feminism is based on Dale O'Leary's informative paper, "Gender: The Deconstruction of Women; Analysis of the Gender Perspective in Preparation for the Fourth World Conference on Women, Beijing, China, September, 1995." Copies are available for $4.00 from Dale O'Leary, P.O. Box 41294, Providence, RI 02940.

16. The papers presented at the Art and Virtual Environments Symposium—held to demonstrate most of the VR art projects sponsored by the Banff Centre 1992–94—are gathered in Moser and MacLeod's *Immersed in Technology.*

17. The quotes in this and the following paragraph are taken from my notes made at the time of presentation.

18. Stone's presentation at 4Cyberconf was a truncated version of the one from which this text has been taken. That presentation, entitled "What Vampires Know: Transsubjection and Transgender in Cyberspace," is available at Stone's World Wide Web site: www.actlab.utexas.edu:80/~sandy/).

19. Ibid.

20. George Lakoff, interviewed by Iain A. Boal, "Body, Brain, and Communication," in James Brook and Iain A. Boal, eds., *Resisting the Virtual Life: The Culture and Politics of Information* (San Francisco: City Light Books, 1995), p. 126.

Chapter 7— Embody the Avatar

1. As the name implies, the creation and development of Habitat was funded by LucasFilm Games, a division of George Lucas's LucasArts Entertainment Company.

2. The Commodore 64 was one of the earliest home computers to sell in any kind of numbers. The "64" in its name referred to the amount of RAM it held, 64K (64,000 bytes)! By comparison, a modern PC typically has 4MB minimum (4 million bytes, or

roughly 60 times the amount of memory in a Commodore 64) with some machines having four, or even eight times that much.

3. See "The Lessons of LucasFilm Habitat," Chip Morningstar and F. Randall Farmer, 1990, a paper presented at The First Annual International Conference on Cyberspace in 1990. It was published in *Cyberspace: First Steps*, Michael Benedikt, ed. (Cambridge: M.I.T. Press, 1990). Available on the Electric Communities World Wide Web site (http://www.communities.com).

4. From "Commerce and Society in Cyberspace, an Electric Communities 'White Paper,' " © 1995 by Electric Communities. Available on the Electric Communities World Wide Web site (http://www.communities.com).

5. Paul Saffo, analyst at the Institute for the Future in Menlo Park, California.   As quoted in Tim Clark, "Putting People in Interactive Computing," *Inter@ctive Week*, 27 November 1995, © 1995 Interactive Enterprises, LLC.

6. Actually cases of mistaken identity—people mistaking computer avatars for human avatars—have already been reported.

7. AlphaWorld home page, 1995 Worlds Inc. (http://www.worlds.net/aworld.html).

Chapter 8—Virtuality and Theophobia

1. See, for example, Carl Raschke, *The Interruption of Eternity: Modern Gnosticism and the Origins of the New Religious Consciousness* (Chicago: Nelson-Hall, 1980); Harold Bloom, *The American Religion: The Emergence of the Post-Christian Nation* (New York: Simon and Schuster, 1992); and Peter Jones, *The Gnostic Empire Strikes Back* (Philipsburg, NJ: Puritan and Reformed Publishing, 1992).

2. David Porush, "Cyberspace: Portal to Transcendence?" *Omni*, April 1993.

3. Eric Davis, "Technopagans" *Wired*, July 1995.

4. Ibid.

5. Ibid.

6. Ibid.

7. Ibid., emphasis added.

8. Ibid.

9. Ibid.

Appendix A

1. Denis De Rougemont, *The Devil's Share*, (New York: Meridian Books, 1944), p. 37.

Appendix B

1. Daniel Akst, "In Cyberspace, Nobody Can Hear You Write a Check," *Los Angeles Times*.

CYBER-GLOSSARY

accelerator—Specialized hardware that increases the speed of graphics manipulation.

accomodation—Change in the focal length of the eye's lens.

actor—A CAD (computer-aided design) representation of a player performing actions for the user, as in the Mandala system. (See "agent," "character," "vactor.")

aesthetics—The philosophy dealing with the human sense of pleasure and artistic merit.

agent—A CAD (computer-aided design) representation of a human form capable of guiding navigators through a virtual reality. (See "actor," "character.")

aliasing—An undesirable jagged edge on many three-dimensional renderings on bitmapped displays. Creates jaggies along the sides of objects and flickering of objects smaller than a pixel (See "anti-aliasing.")

allocentric—That which is other than egocentric, such as a bird's-eye view, or adopting another person's viewpoint.

altered states—The psychology of changes in perception and other states of consciousness that result from changes in external and internal stimulation.

alternate world disorder—Range of discomfort from mild headaches and disorientation to nausea as a result of participating in virtual reality ("barfogenic zone"). (See also "simulator sickness.")

ambient light—General nondirectional illumination.

Archie—A utility that can be used to search for files on FTP (file transfer protocol) sites.

articulation—Objects composed of several parts that are separably moveable.

artificial intelligence—The attempt to mimic and automate human cognitive skills through rules and knowledge representation techniques (for example, understanding visual images, recognizing speech and written text, solving problems, making medical diagnoses, and so forth).

artificial life—Digital agents that evolve, reproduce, grow, and change in similar ways to biological life-forms.

artificial reality—A term introduced by arts and computer visualization scholar Myron Krueger in the mid-1970s to describe his computer-generated responsive environments. He has emphasized the nonintrusive ("second-person virtual reality") systems that track people with pattern recognition techniques and display them and their surroundings on projection systems (see "cave"). Artificial reality involves a computer display system that perceives and captures "a participant's action in terms of the body's relationship to a graphic world and generates responses (usually imagery) that maintain the illusion that his actions are taking place within that world." (See also "virtual reality" and "cyberspace.")

aspect ratio—Ratio of width to height of the field of view.

augmented reality—Involves the use of transparent displays worn as glasses on which data can be projected. This allows someone to repair a radar, for example, and have the needed data displayed in the glasses while walking around the radar.

avatar—A person's likeness, image, or "puppet" in the virtual reality.

back clipping plane—A distance beyond which objects are not shown on the display.

backface removal—The elimination of those polygons that are facing away from the viewer.

backward raytracing—Tracing the path of light from the eye to the object (currently how most raytracing is done).

bandwidth—A measurement of how much data can be transmitted through a line during a given period of time.

binaural—Stereo sound.

biosensors—Special glasses or bracelets containing electrodes to monitor muscle electrical activity.

bodysuit—A complete human covering with virtual reality sensors and effectors. (See "datasuit.")

BOOM—Binocular omni-orientational monitor. A three-dimensional display device suspended from a weighted boom that can swivel freely about so the viewer doesn't have to wear a head mounted display; instead, it steps up to the viewer like a pair of binoculars. The boom's position communicates the user's point of view to the computer.

browser—Overviews such as indexes, lists, or animated maps that enable one to navigate through the physical, temporal, and conceptual elements of a virtual reality.

CAVE—A virtual reality using projection devices on the walls and ceiling to give the illusion of immersion.

character—A being with a virtual body in virtual reality. (See "agent," "vactor.")

chat—Involves sending messages back and forth to someone in real time, usually to a "chat-room" on the Internet.

concept map—A browser containing terms, definitions, and/or icons arranged in semantic proximity.

convergence—The angle between the two eyes at a fixation point. This changes for objects at varying depths in the real world and on three-dimensional displays.

convolvotron—A system for controlling binaural sound production in a virtual reality.

consensual reality—The world, or a simulation of a world, as viewed and comprehended by a society.

cyberia—An Autodesk project and the first virtual reality project by a CAD (computer-aided design) company. (See "cyberspace.")

cybernaut—A voyager in virtual reality.

cybernetic simulation—Dynamic model of a world filled with objects that exhibit lesser or greater degrees of intelligence.

cyberpunk—A dystopian vision of the future, replete with technological dazzle, anomie, and jacked-in cybernauts. A modern literary style.

cyberscope—A viewer that can be attached to a monitor to enable stereoscopic viewing of software-controlled images.

cyberspace—1) A place filled with virtual "stuff" populated by people with virtual bodies. A special kind of virtual space that promotes experiences involving the whole body; 2) A term coined by William Gibson in his book *Neuromancer* to describe a shared virtual universe or "matrix" operating within the sum total of all the world's computer networks. (See also "artificial reality" and "virtual reality.")

cyberspace playhouse—Social center or place where people can go to play roles in simulations.

dataglove—A glove wired with sensors and connected to a computer system for gesture recognition. It is used for tactile feedback and enables navigation through a virtual environment and interaction with three-dimensional objects within it.

dataspace—A visualized representation of complex information.

datasuit—Same as a "dataglove," but designed for the entire body. Only one datasuit has been built, and that with limited capabilities.

deck—A physical space containing an array of instruments that enable a player to act within, and feel a part of, a virtual space.

depth cuing—Involves the use of shading, texture, color, interposition (or many other visual characteristics) to provide a cue for the z-coordinates or distance of an object.

de-rez—Techniques to make pixels less visible in a display.

detail texture—A texture superimposed on another to increase the apparent resolution of the original texture image. Used when the eyepoint is so close to the textured object that the base texture is being magnified. A detail texture, typically a noise image, is blended into the image at a higher resolution adding a gritty realism to the appearance of the object.

direct manipulation—A term coined to reflect the use of computer icons or text as if they were real objects.

disorientation—Confusion about distances and directions for navigation.

droid—A puppet that embodies a human intellect (as in an android).

DSI—Defense Simulation Internet: A component of the Internet that supports DIS (distributed interactive simulations) and SIMNET, and permits scheduled guaranteed bandwidth.

dynamic lighting—Changes in lighting effects on objects as they and the observer move.

dynamics—The way objects interact and move; the rules that govern all actions and behaviors within the environment.

effectors—Output techniques that communicate a user's movements or commands to the computer and to the virtual reality.

egocenter—The sense of self and personal viewpoint that determines one's location in a virtual reality.

Electronic Cafe International (CAFE is an acronym for Communications Access For Everyone)—This concept was born when the Los Angeles Museum of Contemporary Art commissioned Sherrie and Kit to create a project for the 1984 Olympic Festival. A telecom link between five diverse ethnic Los Angeles communities and the museum was maintained for the seven weeks of the festival. It allowed users to trade video and still images, collaborate in writing and drawing on a common virtual canvas, transmit musical pieces, retrieve information, and communicate in dynamic, yet nonaggressive ways. With more advanced equipment and alliances, the ECI is now able to provide a virtual collaborative and real space for anyone to interact with the global village.

e-mail—Electronic mail, often sent over the Internet or a commercial carrier.

endoscopic—Part of a family of new surgical procedures that avoid cutting open major portions of the patient in favor of making small holes through which tools and sensors are inserted and the surgery performed. In a virtual reality or "telepresence" application, the surgeon manipulates the tools by observing the surgery site on a monitor via optical fibers and a tiny video camera.

environment—A computer-generated model that can be experienced from the "inside" as if it were a place.

exoskeletal devices—In order to provide force feedback, designers have added these rigid external supports to gloves and arm motion systems.

eyeball in the hand—A metaphor for visualized tracking where the tracker is held in the hand and is connected to motion of the projection point of the display.

EyeGen—A HMD (head mounted display) made by Virtual Research that combines visual and auditory displays.

Eyephone—A HMD (head mounted display) made by VPL Research that combines visual and auditory displays.

eye tracking—Involves devices that measure the direction of one's gaze. Most HMDs (head mounted displays) do not currently support eye tracking directly.

field of view (FOV)—The angle in degrees of the visual field. Most HMDs (head mounted displays) offer 60 to 90 degrees FOV. Since our two eyes have overlapping 140 degree FOV, binocular or total FOV is roughly 180 degrees horizontal by 120 degrees vertical in most people. A feeling of immersion seems to arise with FOV greater than 60 degrees. (See also "geometric field of view.")

Finger—A command that enables one to inquire about another Internet user.

flame—A hostile electronic message, usually sent to someone who has posted an inappropriate message on-line.

force feedback—The computer guides a machine to offer just the degree of resistance to motion or pressure that a situation would offer in real life; representations of the inertia or resistance objects have when they are moved or touched.

fractal—Any function that contains elements of self-similarity. Often used for fast texture modeling for mountains, trees, clouds, and so forth.

frustum of vision—Three-dimensional field of view in which all modeled objects are visible.

FTP—File transfer protocol; a means of sending and receiving documents and programs over the Internet.

gateway—An electronic pipeline between different computer networks.

geometric field of view (FOVg)—The angle in degrees of the computed visual scene. Most HMDs (head mounted displays) offer 60 to 90 degrees FOV (field of vision), but the scene can be computed to fit into anything from 0 to 360 degrees FOV for any particular projection point. If FOVg is larger than the FOV, then objects will appear pincushioned and distorted; if FOVg is smaller than the FOV, then objects will appear barreled and distorted.

gesture—Hand motion that can be interpreted as a sign, signal, or symbol.

GIF—Graphic interchange format. This picture format is common to on-line graphics.

goggles—Often used to refer to a HMD (head mounted display) or other displays.

Gopher—A software tool that uses menus to navigate the Internet.

gouraud—Shading polygons smoothly with bilinear interpolation.

haptic interfaces—Interfaces that use all the physical sensors that provide us with a sense of touch at the skin level and force feedback information from our muscles and joints.

head-coupled—Displays or robotic actions that are activated by head motion through a head tracking device.

head related transfer function—A mathematical transformation of sound spectrum that modifies the amplitude and phase of acoustic signals to take into account the shape effects of the listener's head.

head tracking—Involves monitoring the position of the head through various devices.

heads up display (HUD)—A display device that lets users see graphics superimposed on their view of the world. (Created for aviators to see symbols and dials while looking out the window.)

hidden surface—Parts of a graphics object occluded by intervening objects.

HMD (head mounted display)—A set of goggles or a helmet with tiny monitors in front of each eye that generate images, seen by the wearer as being three-dimensional. VPL Research refers to their HMDs as eyephones.

holodeck—Virtual reality simulation system used primarily for entertainment by the crew of the starship Enterprise in the *Star Trek: The Next Generation* television series.

HOOD—Swinging wraparound display. Used instead of a HMD (head mounted display); hung from pulleys.

HTML—Hypertext mark-up language. Used to design interlinking "pages" on the World Wide Web.

hypermedia—The combination of digital text, video, and sound with navigation techniques such as buttons, links, and hotspots into one system.

hyperspace—The space of hypertext or hypermedia documents.

hypertext—A means of linking information based on key words.

immersion—The cognitive conviction or feeling of presence—of "being there"—surrounded by space and capable of interacting with all available objects in a virtual reality.

impressionists—A nineteenth-century group of artists whose paintings were directed at capturing color and mood, rather than exact perspective outlines.

interactive fiction—Dramatic creations that encourage user and viewer participation through computer technology.

interface—A set of devices, software, and techniques that connect computers with people to make it easier to perform useful activities.

Internet—A worldwide digital network.

IRC—Internet relay chat.

jack (or "jack in")—To connect to the matrix of virtual space. (See William Gibson's *Necromancer*.)

joystick—Graphic interface device (invented by aviators).

keyframe animation—A process involving interpolating images between stored frames. Also known as "sequence." (See "tweening.")

kinaesthetic dissonance—Mismatch between feedback or its absence from touch or motion during virtual reality experiences.

kinesthesia—The sensation of position or movement.

lag—Delay between an action and its visual, acoustic, or other sensory feedback, often because of inherent delays in the tracking devices, or in the computation of the scene.

laparoscopy (laparoscopic surgery)—Less invasive forms of surgery that operate through small optics and instruments, lending themselves to robotic manipulation and virtual reality training.

LBE (location-based entertainment)—A virtual reality game that involves a scenario based on another time and place.

LCD (liquid crystal display)—Display devices that use bipolar films sandwiched between thin panes of glass. They are lightweight and transmissive or reflective, ideal for a HMD (head-mounted display).

LOD (level of detail)—A model of a particular resolution among a series of models of the same object. Multiple LODs are used to increase graphics performance by drawing simpler geometry when the object occupies fewer pixels on the screen. LOD selection can also be driven by graphics load, area-of-interest, or gaze direction.

magic wand—A three-dimensional interface device used for pointing and interaction; an elongated three-dimensional mouse.

mailing list—A topical discussion held through e-mail on the Internet.

metaball—A kind of "equipotential surface" around a point. You specify a point, a radius, and an "intensity" for each ball; when balls come close, their shapes blend to form a smooth equipotential surface. They seem to be very useful for modeling shapes like animals and humans. They can be rendered by most raytracing packages (also "blobs" or "soft spheres" or "fuzzyspheres").

metaphysics—The philosophical study of basic concepts of existence such as aesthetics, ontology, epistemology, and the meaning and purpose of life.

microsurgery—A form of surgery that lends itself to robotics and virtual reality. (See also "laparoscopy.")

MIDI—A digital sound standard for music.

mirror worlds—Bird's-eye views of a virtual reality in which the viewer also exists and can be seen.

monitor—Display, head mounted display, goggles, liquid crystal display. All computer screens are monitors.

MOO—A MUD (Multiuser dungeon) that is object-oriented. (See also "MUD.")

MOOD—Monoscopic omni-orientational display. (See also "HOOD," "HMD," "goggles," "LCD.")

motion parallax—Objects at different distances and fixation points move different amounts when the viewpoint is dollied along the x-axis (left-right).

motion platform—A controlled system that provides real motion to simulate the displayed motion in a virtual reality.

MRI—Magnetic resonance imaging; a way of making internal organs and structures visible by analyzing radio frequency emissions of atoms in a strong magnetic field. Can be made three-dimensional with rendering of large amounts of data.

MUD—A Multiuser dungeon; a place on the Internet where people can meet and browse (see "MOO").

multiperson space—1) Multiplayer space involving two or more human players; 2) A type of interactive simulation that gives every user a sense that he or she, personally, has a body in virtual space.

multiplayer space—Cyberspace that emerges from a simulation generated simultaneously by two or more decks. Players can be made up of one human and the rest artificial intelligence.

nanomanipulation—Ability to visualize and affect objects in the nanometer range (extremely small).

navigation—Moving through virtual space without losing one's way.

netiquette—Network etiquette.

NetNews—Topical discussion groups found on the Internet.

neural interface—A version of the ultimate interface that connects a virtual reality directly to a human brain or nervous system.

newsgroup—A topical discussion group found on USENET.

newsreader—A software program that allows users to post and retrieve messages on USENET.

objects—Graphical entities that can be dynamically created or loaded from model files. Many functions act upon them:

Tasks—each object performs a specific function per frame; *Hierarchies*—objects can be "linked" together; *Sensors*—objects can be connected to sensors; *Modify*—color, texture, scale, and so forth; *Collision Detection*—between objects and polygons; *Vertices*—these can be dynamically created along with the definition of a vector normal for Gouraud-shading.

occipital cortex—The back of the brain receiving retinotopic projections of visual displays.

occlusion—Hiding objects from sight by the interposition of other objects.

ontology—The metaphysics of existence.

pan—The angular displacement of a view along any axis or direction in a three-dimensional world; or a move through translation in a two-dimensional world.

parietal cortex—The area of the brain adjacent to and above the occipital cortex, thought to process spatial location and direction.

paths—Objects or viewpoints can follow predefined paths that can be dynamically created and interpolated.

perspective—Rules that determine the relative size of objects on a flat page to give the impression of three-dimensional distance.

phong shading—A method for calculating the brightness of a surface pixel by linearly interpolating points on a polygon and using the cosine of the viewing angle. Produces realistic shading.

photorealism—An attempt to create realistic images with much detail and texture.

pitch—The angular displacement of a view along the lateral axis (front-back).

pixel—The smallest element of a display that can be adjusted in intensity.

polygons—An ordered set of vertices connected by sides. These can be dynamically created and texture-mapped using various sources of image data. Various hardware platforms support different texturing methods and quantities. Rendering is performed in either wireframe, smooth-shaded, or textured modes.

pop—When an object's visible appearance suddenly changes or an object appears out of nowhere. Usually an undesired artifact of poor LOD (level of detail).

portals—Polygons that, once passed through, automatically load a new world or execute a user-defined function.

PPP—Point-to-point protocol; used for dial-up connections to the Internet.

presence—A defining characteristic of a good virtual reality system; a feeling of being there, immersed in the environment, able to interact with other objects there.

projected reality—A virtual reality system that uses projection screens rather than HMDs (head mounted displays) or personal display monitors. (See "real projection.")

puppet—An "avatar" or other virtual reality object that can be manipulated.

raytracing—A rendering system that traces the path of light from objects to light sources. (See "backward raytracing.")

real projection—A virtual reality projection system (a pun on rear projection).

real-time—Appearing to be without lag or flicker.

render—Convert a graphics object into pixels.

resolution—Usually the number of lines or pixels in a display—for example, a VGA display has 640 by 480 pixels.

roll—The angular displacement of a view along the longitudinal axis (left-right).

scan conversion—The change of video signals from one form (for example, RGB) to another (for example, NTSC, PAL).

scintillation—The "sparkling" of textures or small objects. Usually undesirable and caused by aliasing.

second person virtual reality—The use of a computational medium to portray a representation of you that is not necessarily realistic, but still identifiable ("puppet", "avatar," "vactor"). In the Mandala system, for example, a video camera allows you to see yourself as another object over which you have control by your own bodily movement.

sensor—A mechanism or function that acts to change objects in response to multiple devices connected to lights, objects, viewpoints, and so forth, in the real world.

sensor lagtime—Delays in the feedback or representation of your actions caused by computation in the tracker or sensor.

sensory substitution—The conversion of sensory information from one sense to another (for example, the use of auditory echoes and cues to "see" the shape of your surroundings).

sequence—Also called "keyframe animation," this involves the interpolation of images between stored frames. (See "tweening.")

shared worlds—Virtual environments that are shared by multiple participants at the same location or across long-distance networks.

shutter glasses—LCD (liquid crystal display) screens or physically rotating shutters used to see stereoscopically when linked to the frame rate of a monitor.

SIMNET—For SIMulator NETworking, the advanced technology development of large scale, fully interactive, widely distributed simulations created by ARPA with significant Army participation and executed by scientists and engineers from BBN and Perceptronics. Begun in 1983, the first networked simulators were operational in the summer of 1986. This program proved the feasibility of real-time, shared synthetic environments, and has resulted in numerous follow-on programs in the Department of Defense as well as in the commercial/entertainment sector (for example, CyberMind and Virtual World). Using networked graphics and displays built into physical mock-ups, it has been called a vehicle-based virtual reality or synthetic environment. (See also "DIS," "DSI.")

simulator sickness—The disturbances produced by simulators, ranging in degree from a feeling of unpleasantness, disorientation, and headaches, to nausea and vomiting. Many factors may be involved, including sensory distortions such as abnormal movement of arms and heads (because of the weight of equipment), long lags in feedback, and missing visual cues from convergence and accommodation. Simulator sickness rarely occurs with displays less than 60 degrees visual angle.

SLIP—Serial line Internet protocol; used for dial-up connections to the Internet.

SMTP—Simple mail transfer protocol; specifies how electronic mail is transferred over the Internet.

spamming—Refers to posting multiple copies of the same message. A violation of netiquette.

spatial navigation—Accurate self-localization and orientation in virtual spaces is not as easy as real-world navigation. Devising techniques for embedding navigational assists in complex dataspaces remains an important research goal.

spatial representation system—The cortical and other neural structures and functions that maintain spatial orientation and recognition.

spatial superposition—Refers to the fact that in augmented reality displays, accurate spatial registration of real and virtual images remains difficult.

striate cortex—Visual cortex. (See "occipital cortex," "parietal cortex.")

supercockpit—An Air Force project led by Tom Furness that advanced the engineering and human factors of HMDs (head mounted displays) and virtual reality. It used digital displays of instruments and terrain.

Sword of Damocles—Nickname for the first helmet mounted display at the University of Utah.

synthetic environments—Virtual reality displays used for simulation.

Sysop—System operator of a computer bulletin board system.

tactile displays—Devices such as force-feedback gloves, buzzers, and exoskeletons that provide tactile, kinaesthetic, and joint sensations. (See also "exoskeletal devices.")

TCP/IP—Transmission control protocol/Internet protocol; a suite of computer protocols that govern how computers exchange information over the Internet.

tele-existence—Remote virtual reality.

telemanipulation—Robotic control of distant objects.

telepresence—Virtual reality with displays of real, remote scenes.

telerobotic—Robotic control of distant objects. (See "telemanipulation," "teleoperation").

telesurgery—Surgery using teleoperation. (See also "laparoscopy.")

Telnet—A means of connecting one's computer to another non-local computer via the Internet.

terrain—Geographical information and models that can be either randomly generated or based on actual data. Dynamic terrain is an important goal for current SIMNET applications.

texture mapping—A bitmap added to an object to give added realism. (See "detail texture.")

texture swimming—Unnatural motion of static textures on the surfaces of objects as they are rotated. Caused by quick and dirty texture interpolation in screen coordinates. Correctable by subdividing polygons or by doing perspective correction.

tracker—A device that emits numeric coordinates for its changing position in space. (See also "enactive tracking.")

transparency—Refers to how invisible and unobtrusive a virtual reality system is.

transterritorial—Beyond physical space, as in cyberspace.

trompe l'oeil—Perspective paintings that deceive viewers into believing they are real (for example, a painting of the sky and clouds on the inside of a dome).

tweening—The interpolation of images between stored frames.

universe—The "container" of all entities in a virtual reality. Entities can be temporarily added or removed from consideration by the simulation manager. The sequence of events in the simulation loop can be user-defined.

URL—Uniform resource locator; the standard addressing method that identifies pages on the World Wide Web.

USENET—A series of topical discussion groups found on the Internet.

vactor—A virtual actor, either autonomous or telerobotic, in a virtual reality theater.

Veronica—Very easy rodent-oriented netwide index to computerized archives; a search utility for the Internet.

viewpoints—Points from which raytracing and geometry creation occur; the geometric eye-point of the simulation. You can have multiple viewpoints that can be attached to multiple sensors.

virtual environments—Realistic simulations of interactive scenes.

virtual patient—Telerobotic or digitized animations of humans with accurate disease models.

virtual prototyping—The use of virtual reality for design and evaluation of new artifacts.

virtual reality—A term coined by Jaron Lanier to describe an immersive, interactive simulation of realistic or imaginary environments.

visualization—Use of computer graphics to make visible numeric or other quantifiable relationships.

voxel—A cubic volume pixel for quantizing three-dimensional space.

WAIS—Wide area information server.

waldo—A remotely controlled mechanical puppet.

WAN—Wide area network; a computer network that encompasses a large geographic area.

windows—On some hardware platforms, you can have multiple windows and viewpoints into the same virtual world.

wire frame outlines—Displays of the outlines of polygons, not filled in.

world—An entire virtual reality environment or universe.

world in the hand—A metaphor for visualized tracking where the tracker is held in the hand and is connected to the motion of the object located at that position in the display.

World Wide Web—A global collection of linked "pages" that utilizes hypertext to navigate from one site to another.

The original version of this "Cyber Glossary" was written by Joe Psotka and Sharon A. Davison. It was revised by Marc Bernatchez, and then edited and adapted by George Otis, Jr. for use at the Compasspoint/Sentinel Seminar, Atlanta, Georgia, November 1996, where Tal Brooke and George Otis were keynote speakers.

For further information:

Benedikt, M., ed., *Cyberspace: First Steps* (Cambridge, MA: The M.I.T. Press, 1991).

Earnshaw, R. A., M.A. Gigante, and H. Jones. *Virtual Reality Systems* (New York: Academic Press, 1993).

Ellis, S. R., ed., *Pictorial Communication in Virtual and Real Environments* (London: Taylor and Francis, 1991).

Heim, M. *The Metaphysics of Virtual Reality* (New York: Oxford University Press, 1993).

Kalawsky, R. *The Science of Virtual Reality and Virtual Environments* (New York: Addison-Wesley, 1993).

Latham, R. *The Dictionary of Computer Graphics Technology and Applications* (New York: Springer-Verlag, 1991).

Laurel, B. *Computers as Theater* (New York: Addison-Wesley, 1991).

Pimentel and Teixeira. *Through the Looking Glass* (Intel, 1992).

Rheingold, H. *Virtual Reality* (New York: Simon & Schuster, 1991).

BIBLIOGRAPHY

Aukstakalnis and Blatner, *Silicon Mirage: The Art and Science of Virtual Reality*. Peach Pit Press, 1992.

Bender, Gretchen and Timothy Rucker, eds. *Culture on the Brink: Ideologies of Technology*. Seattle: Bay Press, 1994.

Bloom, Harold. *The American Religion: The Emergence of the Post-Christian Nation*. New York: Simon and Schuster, 1992.

Brook, James and Iain A. Boal, eds. *Resisting the Virtual Life: The Culture and Politics of Information*. San Francisco: City Light Books, 1995.

Bukatman, Scott. *Terminal Identity: The Virtual Subject in Postmodern Science Fiction*. Durham: Duke University Press, 1993.

De Kerckhove, Derrick. *The Skin of Culture: Investigating the New Electronic Reality*. Toronto: Somerville House Publishing, 1995.

De Rougemont, Denis. *The Devil's Share*. New York: Meridian Books, 1944.

Ehrenfeld, David. *The Arrogance of Humanism*. New York: Oxford University Press, 1978.

Ellul, Jacques. *The Technological Bluff*. Grand Rapids: Eerdmans, 1990.

Ellul, Jacques. *The Technological Society*. New York: Vintage Books, 1964.

Gergen, Kenneth J. *The Saturated Self: Dilemmas of Identity in Contemporary Life*. New York: Basic Books, 1992.

Jones, Peter. *The Gnostic Empire Strikes Back*. Philipsburg: Puritan and Reformed Publishing, 1992.

Juenger, Freidrich Georg. *The Failure of Technology*. Chicago: Henry Regnery, 1949.

Kroker, Arthur and Michael Weinstein. *Data Trash: The Theory of the Virtual Class*. New York: St. Martin's Press, 1994.

Lochhead, David. *Theology in a Digital World*. Canada: The United Church Publishing House, 1988.

Lukacs, John. *The End of the Twentieth Century and the End of the Modern Age*. New York: Ticknor & Fields, 1993.

Mander, Jerry. *Four Arguments for the Elimination of Television*. New York: William Morrow, 1978.

McLuhan, Marshall. *Understanding Media: The Extensions of Man*. New York: McGraw-Hill, 1964.

Mitchell, William J. *City of Bits: Space, Place, and the Infobahn*. Cambridge: The M.I.T. Press, 1995.

Moravec, Hans. *Mind Children: The Future of Robot and Human Intelligence*. Cambridge: Harvard University Press, 1988.

Moser, Mary Anne and Douglas MacLeod, eds. *Immersed in Technology: Art and Virtual Environments*. Cambridge: The M.I.T. Press, 1996.

Muggerage, Malcolm. *Christ and the Media*. Grand Rapids: Eerdmans, 1977.

Raschke, Carl. *The Interruption of Eternity: Modern Gnosticism and the Origins of the New Religious Consciousness*. Chicago: Nelson-Hall, 1980.

Rheingold, Howard. *The Virtual Community: Homesteading on the Electronic Frontier*. Reading, MA: Addison Wesley Publishing Company, 1993.

Rushkoff, Douglas. *Cyberia: Life in the Trenches of Hyperspace*. New York: HarperCollins, 1994.

Schwartau, Winn. *Information Warfare: Chaos on the Electronic Superhighway*. New York: Thunder's Mouth Press, 1994.

Stoll, Clifford. *Silicon Snake Oil: Second Thoughts on the Information Highway*. New York: Doubleday, 1995.

Toffler, Alvin. *Future Shock*. New York: Random House, 1970.

Veith, Gene Edward. *Postmodern Times: A Christian Guide to Contemporary Thought and Culture*. Wheaton: Crossway Books, 1994.

Walsh, Brian J. and J. Richard Middleton. *The Transforming Vision: Shaping a Christian World View*. Downers Grove: InterVarsity Press, 1984.

Weiner, Norbert. *Cybernetics*. Cambridge: The M.I.T. Press, 1948.

Weiner, Norbert. *God and Golem, Inc.* Cambridge: The M.I.T. Press, 1964.

Wurman, Richard Saul. *Information Anxiety*. New York: Doubleday, 1989.

Zerzan, John and Alice Carnes, eds. *Questioning Technology: Tool, Toy or Tyrant?* Philadelphia: New Society Publishers, 1991.

When the World Will Be As One

— THE NEXT PHASE —

Beyond the New Age Movement

by Tal Brooke

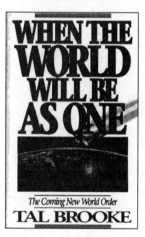

In recent years the New Age movement has been touted by many as the spiritual rebirth of modern man. But this popular movement is just one phase of a broad agenda which is only now coming fully into view. The pieces have been shifting into place for a quantum leap more radical than the one that replaced the Dark Ages with the Age of Reason. A momentous global event is upon us—the birth of a New World Order.

LINCOLN CHRISTIAN COLLEGE AND SEMINARY
SPIRITUAL COUNTERFEITS PROJECT

Tal Brooke is president of Spiritual Counterfeits Project (SCP), a nationwide ministry. SCP's core staff is from top-ranked universities and have each traveled various spiritual paths before becoming Christians.

SCP's major publication is the *SCP Journal*, which has won three first-place EPA awards. This in-depth publication explores the latest deceptive spiritual trends such as near-death experiences, deep ecology, UFOs, and the Jesus Seminar, and exposes their inside workings from a biblical perspective. SCP also publishes the *SCP Newsletter* four times a year with the latest news and developments on the spiritual frontlines.

The SCP Journal and *SCP Newsletter* are sent to those who contribute at least $25 annually ($35 outside the USA). The newsletter is available separately for a $10 annual donation (to offset publication, printing, and postage costs).

- -

SCP, Inc.

Box 4308, Berkely, CA 94704
Business Office: (510) 540-0300
ACCESS Line: (510) 540-5767
Web Site: http://www.scp-inc.org

Enclosed is a gift of $25 or more—please send me the *SCP Journal* and *SCP Newsletter*.

Name _____

Phone _____

Address _____

City _____ State _____ Zip Code _____